BAZAAR STYLE

Decorating with market and vintage finds

Selina Lake

with words by Joanna Simmons

photography by Debi Treloar

Designers Amy Trombat & Paul Stradling
Editors Clare Double & Rebecca Woods
Location Research Selina Lake & Jess Walton
Production Toby Marshall
Editorial Director Julia Charles
Art Director Leslie Harrington

Styling Selina Lake

First published in 2008
This edition published in 2013
by Ryland Peters & Small
20—21 Jockey's Fields
London WC1R 4BW
and
519 Broadway, 5th Floor
New York, NY 10012
www.rylandpeters.com

Text copyright © Joanna Simmons 2008, 2013
Design and photographs copyright
© Ryland Peters & Small 2008, 2013

10 9 8 7 6 5 4 3 2 1

ISBN: 978 1 84975 366 1

A CIP record from this book is
available from the British Library.

This book was previously catalogued as follows:

Lake, Selina.
 Bazaar style : decorating with market and vintage
finds / Selina Lake ; photography by Debi Treloar ;
with words by Joanna Simmons.
-- 1st U.S. ed.
  p. cm.
 Includes index.
 ISBN 978-1-84597-626-2
1. Found objects (Art) in interior decoration.
2. Antiques in interior decoration. I. Title.
NK2115.5.F68L35 2008
747--dc22
                              2007038244

Printed and bound in China.

CONTENTS

INTRODUCTION

From a Turkish market with hundreds of stalls groaning under the weight of fabrics, spices and trinkets, to a village fair selling everything from homemade jam to second-hand books, bazaars the world over are all about abundance. There's plenty to see and much to delight the senses. Bazaar style encapsulates all this colour, richness and diversity – and brings it home. The look is relaxed and individual, with rooms that are comfortable, maybe a little quirky, but always full of interest.

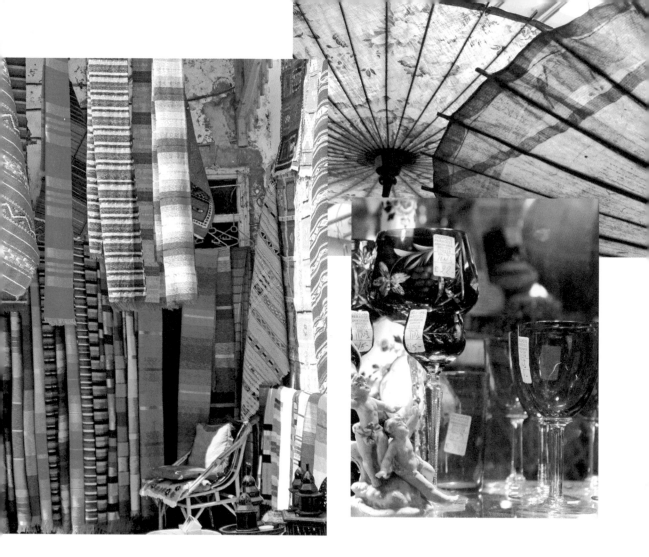

Bazaar style is the antidote to interiors magazines listing must-have products and the latest colours. It doesn't follow fashion or obey rules, but allows you to set your imagination free, mixing furniture and fabrics from across the decades. It's a look that is easy to pull off because anything goes, from vintage and retro to recycled and restored. There's no snobbery in a bazaar-style home. Pieces inherited from a great-aunt can be cherished alongside something found on a foreign holiday. No item is off-limits, either. Shabby objects can be quickly refreshed – a lick of white eggshell paint can transform a tired dresser, or a row of sequins rev up a plain cushion.

Flea markets, boot fairs, antiques shops and eBay are rich hunting grounds, all offering an element of surprise – you never know what you're going to find. From foreign treasures such as French linen tablecloths to English country classics like floral tea sets and rustic baskets. From retro wallpapers to Welsh woollen blankets, oil paintings to old mirrors. Pieces that have lived long or travelled far come with personality built in. A lantern that you haggled for in a foreign market; a neglected chair you found in a French *brocante* fair; a frayed throw you nursed back to life with needle and thread; these items will give your home life and soul. How much nicer to have a rug created using traditional artisan techniques than a factory-made alternative? How much more interesting to have furniture that tells a story than a mass-produced flat-pack piece, cheap to buy, but hard to value?

The bazaar look cannot be bought on one shopping trip. It grows organically over the years, with finds gathered from diverse sources. It celebrates the beauty of our everyday possessions, too – almost anything can look striking when thoughtfully arranged and given room to breathe – and loves colour. Think of the rich tones of Moroccan kilims on a souk stall, the flowers in a Dutch market or the colours on the spines of old paperbacks in a second-hand bookshop. Colour used bravely and abundantly can inspire, refresh and invigorate the senses. Most of us feel better with some colour in our lives.

Bazaar Style will show you where to shop, what to look for and how to put it all together. There is a wealth of inspiration to be found in the interiors shown on these pages, and by seeing what others have done in their homes you'll gain confidence to experiment in yours. Perhaps you have never dared hang a floral painting, picked up in a junk shop, against flowery wallpaper or had not guessed that granny's old toby jug could look so good as a vase. You might not have thought of showing off your jewellery in a beautiful old teacup, or keeping kitchen crockery in an old wardrobe. By absorbing the unusual combinations and innovative ways in which everyday objects have been made to look exceptional, you'll begin to master a whole new style. Happily, it's one that need not cost much and isn't hard to achieve. Just have fun and follow your instincts.

elements

FURNITURE
and STORAGE

From an antique chaise longue recovered in lush velvet to a swivelling Sixties chair picked up in a market, furniture that shouts individuality is key to the bazaar look. The odd modern classic or simple piece bought on the high street may find its way into a bazaar-style home, but generally its rooms are stuffed with furniture that has seen a bit of life and has the personality to prove it.

ABOVE LEFT *A humble chest of drawers offers invaluable storage and looks good in almost any room. Paint a tired pine piece white to refresh it, then create a display of collectables on top. A feathered wall decoration, hanging above, provides a shot of glamour, too.*

BELOW LEFT *Shoes are objects of beauty in their own right, so enjoy their colours and design when you're not wearing them by arranging them on open shelves.*

OPPOSITE *Books add life to any room, but don't need to be neatly lined up on conventional shelves, library-style. Here, a clear perspex unit is home to a collection of large hardbacks.*

The joy of buying second-hand is that you have so much choice. A modern furniture store will sell beds, sofas, armchairs, tables – formulaic pieces designed for a single purpose. Go shopping for old furniture, however, think laterally, and a world of options opens up. First, there's the exciting surprise element – you cannot predict what will take your fancy, from a French wrought-iron daybed to a slim Seventies sideboard. Then, if you consider how objects meant for one function can be adapted to another, further opportunities present themselves. A hospital trolley can work as a side table; a department store display cabinet can be a cavernous chest of drawers; an old tea chest makes a good TV stand.

Second-hand pieces are, by definition, old and well used, but that doesn't mean their quality has been compromised. They were often made using skills and materials rarely found in today's mass-produced furniture industry. You may have

to give them a makeover, but you're getting a piece made with care and expertise, already proven to have stood the test of time, and often at a bargain price. Buying second-hand is ethical, too, sitting comfortably with today's emphasis on recycling and reusing. With so much enticing, good-quality furniture out there already, why buy new?

Junk shops, house clearance sales and flea markets are good sources of interesting second-hand furniture. Internet auction sites such as eBay also offer rich pickings, but make sure you check the measurements of any item carefully before you bid. It is easy to get carried away, only to bid successfully on a piece that will not fit anywhere in your home or looks disappointingly small when it arrives. Weigh up delivery and transport costs, too – you may be able to afford something more expensive if it's local.

The bazaar look is not necessarily about buying everything cheaply, however. You may want to blow

THIS PAGE *We often rely on collectables and art to add colour and decoration to a room, but a show-stopping armchair brings drama that you can curl up in. The owner found it in a skip and had it painted and upholstered in crimson.*

OPPOSITE LEFT *This La Chaise chair by Charles and Ray Eames is a modern classic. Its white fibreglass shell and modernist design look even more striking set against a contrasting bazaar-style backdrop of patterned wallpaper.*

OPPOSITE RIGHT *Sensual velvet makes a wonderful upholstery fabric and these cute armchairs, covered in brilliant pink, feel as good as they look. Different floral patterns have been layered on in this living space, but a colour theme of rich pink unites the scheme.*

RIGHT *An elegant French armchair, found in a charity shop, is given a feminine makeover with pink paint on its frame and patterned silk upholstery.*

OPPOSITE, ABOVE LEFT *This ornate armchair has been reborn in striking style with a metallic painted frame and black upholstery.*

OPPOSITE, ABOVE RIGHT *Retro orange leather chairs with tubular frames are softened with patterned and animal-hide cushions.*

OPPOSITE, BELOW LEFT *This sofa is covered with a fabric by Marimekko. Printed with branches and leaves, rather than a repeat pattern, it makes the sofa look like a piece of art.*

OPPOSITE, BELOW RIGHT *A green leather and metal armchair is an eye-catching addition to this living space. A backdrop of glossy black painted floorboards and white walls is all it needs to look its best.*

the budget on a fabulous designer chair, but find the rest of your living-room furniture in flea markets. A contemporary item or design classic will look doubly arresting alongside painted furniture and squashy sofas than in the more predictable setting of a modernist room. It is the combination of objects that makes a bazaar-style scheme exciting, so buy something because you love it, not because it matches what you already own. Passion for the piece is all that matters.

When hunting for big pieces of furniture like sofas and chairs, you will be drawn to their style first, but you should also look at how they are made. A solid wooden frame and a well-sprung, comfortable seat with stuffing intact are important – putting these right is expensive. Reupholstering,

on the other hand, is easier to do and, while reasonably costly, allows you to hand-pick a fabric that will fit the space perfectly. A cheap alternative is to layer a worn sofa, chaise or chair with throws, old linen sheets or tactile lambskins to refresh its appearance, or have simple loose covers made. When it comes to beds, think about combining old and new for a happy marriage of style and comfort. An old wooden or iron frame looks great, and when teamed with a new mattress you get a bed that feels wonderful, too.

Remember to look beyond appearances to see each item's full potential. That way, you will have the pick of the pieces that others overlook. Wonky hinges and missing knobs can be replaced on wardrobes, cupboards and cabinets. Varnish can

ABOVE LEFT *This filing cabinet was once grey, but has been reinvented with floral paper, stuck to its drawers. It makes a lively contrast to the simple wooden shelving.*

ABOVE RIGHT *Displaying ordinary things and enjoying their beauty is an idea at the heart of bazaar style, and in this kitchen a simple glass-fronted unit allows its brightly coloured inhabitants to be appreciated.*

be stripped and some nourishing wax used in its place for a fresh look. The most dreary armchair can look outstanding when newly covered with a retro fabric or plush velour, and bright paint can do much to disguise the unexciting shape of a wooden bookshelf or chest of drawers.

When it comes to storage, built-in units and cupboards can make the most of an awkward corner or create storage in an unlikely location (above a door, say, or under the stairs), but they can be expensive to have specially made and, of course, cannot travel with you when you move. You may prefer to opt for freestanding pieces instead, or a mixture of both. In a kitchen, an old wardrobe makes a roomy home for china, while wall-hung units can store food. In the bedroom, open shelves can hold shoes and bags, and a built-in wardrobe house clothes.

Remember, too, that bazaar-style homes celebrate the beauty in everyday objects, so don't hide all your possessions behind sleek cupboard doors: have most of them on show, but organized; visible, but ordered. To do this, look for versatile storage such as wicker baskets, glass-fronted cabinets, shelves, wooden fruit or wine crates, ex-shop furniture, trolleys and hooks. Use them to store everything from towels to teacups, clothes to crockery.

For those possessions which do need to be stored out of sight, there are plenty of pieces that provide practicality with personality. An old plan chest or wooden filing cabinet can keep unattractive paperwork, folders or stationery tidy and hidden away. Suitcases, metal trunks, wooden boxes, Lloyd Loom linen baskets and chunky old pine chests make regular appearances at markets and fairs and

ABOVE LEFT *Wooden dressers are chunky classics, teaming practical storage with open shelves for display. The painting by Jenny Jones depicts the house owners on their wedding day.*

ABOVE RIGHT *Teaming an oversized Anglepoise lamp with traditional pieces – a chandelier and pretty china – gives this dining space a sense of humour. Playing with scale and mixing styles is central to bazaar style.*

ABOVE LEFT *Shoes and handbags arranged on open shelves look like an art installation and give a room lots of personality.*

ABOVE RIGHT *Bazaar style is not about keeping your possessions behind closed doors. Here, a simple unit is home to colourful baskets and shoes, bringing visual interest, colour and texture to the room.*

OPPOSITE *The patterned textiles and reclaimed furniture give this teenager's bedroom a laid-back, pretty look. The blackboard paint on the walls allows her to chalk up her own art. The lampshade is made from old buttons and the curtains from towelling. A found shop display cabinet is now used as a chest of drawers.*

offer ample, good-looking storage – throw kids' toys, dirty laundry or muddy boots into them and close the lid. For those smaller items that need stashing away or organizing neatly, sniff around for old tins, jars, boxes, drawers and hampers. Once you start looking, creative storage solutions are everywhere!

ABOVE *A floral theme links the faded fabric of this sofa with the vibrant cushions. The embroidered sunflowers introduce lashings of texture.*

RIGHT *A mismatched combination of sheets, quilts and pillowcases gives this bed a relaxed, pretty look. By layering the bedding, no single pattern is allowed to dominate, but all have a chance to shine.*

OPPOSITE *Two different patterns coexist happily here. The wallpaper is traditional, while the cushion, made from vintage fabric remnants, is unmistakably Seventies. By sitting the cushion on a chair of similar colour, the eye is drawn to them, while the wallpaper mellows into the background.*

TEXTILES

Curtains, upholstery, throws, bedding, cushions – textiles crop up in every room of the house and can bring it beautifully to life. They marry texture, pattern and colour, three essential ingredients of bazaar style, and can take an interior from ordinary to individual in an instant. The trick is to team a variety of textiles together to create a rich visual and sensual mix.

Introducing textiles into any scheme is quick and inexpensive. In a living room, mix and match cushions, bringing in new ones and rotating old as you fancy. Use fabric remnants to make a relaxed throw or customize a simple shop-bought cushion by stitching on sequins, tassels or felt flowers. In a bedroom, ditch the matching bedlinen in favour of a muddle of pretty patterns on duvets/comforters, bedspreads and pillowcases, picked up at markets or second-hand stores. Hang delicate vintage lace at a window to diffuse the light and add rich damask curtains for privacy at night. Wake up an old coffee table or bedside cabinet by covering it with a length of fabric, then top it off with a pane of glass, cut to fit at your local glazier. In your work space, use an old linen tablecloth or a thick Indian bedspread to cover a tired desk. If your workstation is in an open-plan living area, create some privacy by sectioning it off with pretty muslin, net curtains or vintage silk scarves pegged together.

The world is your shopping oyster when you're looking for textiles that suit the bazaar look. Ethnic shops are excellent hunting grounds for jewel-bright sari fabric, swatches of shimmering Thai silk or Moroccan rugs and bedspreads in spicy colours. Flea markets will generally have a selection of old rugs that, when professionally cleaned, can look superb, alongside plenty of fabric offcuts of all types of material, old curtains and clothes. Try eBay for original fabrics from every decade of the 20th century and don't rule out reproduction fabrics, either – many shops (including those chain stores on the high street) sell scatter cushions and lampshades in prints inspired by Seventies

psychedelia or vintage florals that look just as good as the real thing.

When you're working textiles into your home, remember to think outside the decorating box. Sari fabric can make a pretty canopy for a bed. Sarongs and shawls make excellent throws for sofas or armchairs, as do old blankets and patchwork quilts. Second-hand curtains can be cut up to make cushion covers, as can old woolly jumpers or vintage dresses and shirts – all you need is a sewing machine and a spare afternoon. A curtain may not offer enough material to make a tablecloth, but it could be reborn as pretty placemats. If you love the pattern of a fabric remnant, frame it for some instant artwork.

The bazaar look often incorporates textiles into a room just for the sheer joy of having them there –

ABOVE LEFT *By picking a floral theme, cushions in a range of different vintage fabrics from across the decades can look wonderful together.*

ABOVE RIGHT *Ethnic textiles are often made with strong, bright, saturated colours. Here, a Moroccan cushion sits against an embroidered Indian throw, their shared palette making them a great team.*

OPPOSITE *Pale walls and plenty of pink and red give this living space energy. Moroccan cushions bring a simple sofa to life, their colour echoed in the paintings above. Artist Ana Drummond made the 'Just Say No Thank You' painting.*

THIS PAGE *This comfortable old sofa in a garden outhouse is layered with blankets, throws and cushions to give it bright and inviting colour and texture. Piling on the textiles has the added benefit of concealing worn seats or frayed upholstery.*

OPPOSITE LEFT *Square floor cushions covered in fantastically bright textiles are a flexible, informal alternative to a traditional sofa. Supplement them with matching cushions that can be propped against the wall to boost comfort and a cosy blanket for relaxed, low-level lounging.*

OPPOSITE RIGHT *A pile of fabric swatches in brilliant colours forms a striking display. Keep them on open shelves or piled in a basket until you are ready to fashion them into cushion covers or throws – or just enjoy them as they are.*

they need not serve a practical purpose. So if you find a delicious swatch of old fabric or a lovely old curtain, hang it against a wall as a tactile artwork or across a doorway as a partition. Tack lengths of delicate lace or strips of patterned fabric above a window or along a tabletop edge. Pin a collection of handkerchiefs or napkins to a wall or door. Pile up fabric remnants, waiting to be fashioned into pillowcases or cushion covers, in an old basket or on a shelf so you can enjoy their colour and pattern before you get to work on them.

There are no rules to displaying textiles, only guidelines. Try layering them, so that garish prints don't dominate. Top a wildly printed bed sheet with a faded quilt to tame it, for example – you still get to enjoy the lively pattern, but it won't walk all over your bedroom. Don't be afraid to clash textiles, either, but reduce the visual shock by finding one unifying element – a key colour or a similar pattern, be that floral, geometric or retro.

Remember to mix in plenty of texture, too. A room that invites you to reach out and touch it is

ABOVE *Fabrics, needlework samplers and knitted blankets – some family heirlooms – have been arranged on a bench, simply to be enjoyed in all their variety.*

RIGHT *Old lace and delicately woven fabrics crop up at markets and fairs regularly and make great window treatments. This lace panel helps provide privacy, while the heavy embroidered fabric that covers the console table below makes a tactile contrast.*

OPPOSITE *An eclectic mix of patterns, textures and textiles lives in this bedroom, from the exotic wallpaper to the floral fabric canopy. The bedspread was made from lengths of traditional Dutch ribbon, painstakingly stitched together.*

more relaxing and welcoming than one that simply looks great. The tactile surprise of finding a silk cushion next to a mohair one, a fake-fur throw next to a cotton one, is pleasing and exciting. Enjoy exploring the range of textures that just one material can offer, too. Wool, for example, can be thick and reassuring in an old Welsh blanket, or incredibly soft and sensual in the form of merino wool from Spain, famous for its extra-long fibres.

THIS PAGE *Colours are bold, blocky and brilliant in this living space. There is very little pattern in the scheme here, but a great deal of strong, bright colour. Neutral walls and glossy black floorboards create a simple backdrop for the huge artwork, graphic cushions and striped rug. It's an unfussy, brave look that works well with the clean lines of the designer furniture.*

OPPOSITE *A graphically patterned rug like the one in this living space becomes the eye-catching chief artwork of the room. Walls are left plain and neutral to let it take centre stage, while a bright orange sofa and lavender stair carpet continue the colourful theme.*

COLOUR
and PATTERN

Throughout history, we have incorporated colour, pattern and decoration into our homes. It is human instinct to decorate and adorn, injecting interest and beauty into our domestic environment. Bazaar style shows you how to use colour and pattern beautifully.

ABOVE *China introduces colour and pattern on a small scale. Here, pretty plates and a tray share a simple floral design and vibrant colours.*

RIGHT *Vintage Seventies wallpaper bought on eBay creates a bold wall of pattern. A sideboard from a charity shop looks perfect in front.*

OPPOSITE LEFT *A colour theme of grey, black and white and a mix of geometric shapes and patterns gives this hallway real drama. Seen from this angle, the mirrored unit reflects the rug's pattern, doubling its impact.*

OPPOSITE RIGHT *Coloured glass bricks make a beautiful room partition and their shades are echoed in the chair and rug beyond.*

In Medieval times, even simple homes were often colourfully painted, using limewash mixed with whatever ingredients were to hand – animal blood or yellow ochre. Fabrics were the usual means of adding colour to Elizabethan rooms, while in the Georgian period (1760–1830) pastel blues and greens were common on walls, made by mixing copper or iron sulphate into the plaster. In the mid-1800s, when wallpaper production was mechanized and it could be cheaply made, everybody was pasting it up. New dyes were developed, too, so designs in bright colours hit Victorian homes, jostling for attention alongside heavy curtains, rich rugs and an abundance of ornaments. Set against this historical context, the recent vogue for paring down, putting away and using pale colours seems a blip, rather than a lasting trend. We have, it seems, always loved colour and pattern.

Paint is an easy and inexpensive way to bring colour into your home. Spend an afternoon emulsioning your walls and you can completely reinvent a room for the price of a few litres. You need not paint every room, or even every wall. To introduce some colour without fear of it dominating, use it as an accent against a neutral backdrop, painting it on a chimney breast or a single wall, or paint the return of the window to frame the view. Paints suitable for woodwork (gloss, satinwood and

eggshell) are now available in a huge range of shades, too, so bring colour to doors, skirting boards and window frames while keeping walls white. Alternatively, paint your floorboards – another effective way to introduce colour without splashing it up the walls.

For a combination of pattern and colour, look to wallpaper. Enjoying a huge style renaissance today, it is available in a range of designs and prices. You can also find original wallpapers from the 20th century – the internet is a good source. Use it as an accent or artwork, by hanging on one wall, in a chimney alcove or inside an old picture frame. Creative types can paste offcuts and samples side by

side for a patchwork effect. And don't stop there – layer on more pattern by hanging a flower painting or an embroidered dress against floral wallpaper. To find the right paper for you, tack up samples before you buy a whole roll and, if you're using an expensive wallpaper or one with a complicated pattern, consider paying a professional to hang it.

Fabric and upholstery are two further sources of colour and pattern and much used in a bazaar-style room. Scatter vibrant cushions and throws over a neutral sofa and layer crocheted blankets, ethnic bedspreads and embroidered sheets on a bed. If you are handy with a needle and thread, use a mish-mash of fabric remnants to make cushion

ABOVE *Really bright colours like this lime green can enliven a room and create a talking point. Temper them with neutral walls and simple furniture.*

RIGHT *In this Moroccan house a scattering of cushions with bold flower designs, made from fabric bought locally, create a vibrant fireside seating area.*

OPPOSITE LEFT *Layering colour and pattern works well in a bazaar-style room. Here, picture frames pick out the pink, red and yellow in the wallpaper, while their neat stripes create a graphic contrast. The paper is by Matthew Williamson for Habitat.*

OPPOSITE RIGHT *A simple arrangement of lamp and vases sits well in front of this large-scale wallpaper pattern (Birdtree by Neisha Crosland). A bigger display could look fussy and chaotic.*

covers or loose covers for sofa and armchair seats —
it's a cheap way to revive a battered piece and inject
plenty of pattern.

When it comes to dressing windows, you'll find
mountains of second-hand curtains at flea markets
and jumble/rummage sales. If the patterns are too
wild or faded, customize them with sections of plain
cotton, or find an alternative; a tablecloth, sheet
or length of lace might do as well. Floors can get
expressive with a colourful, pattern-rich rug. Go
ethnic with a spice-toned dhurri from India, retro
with a Seventies swirly design, or choose a more
organic look with fake zebra-print hides or woven
seagrass. Move them from room to room, layer
them or let them peep out from under chairs and

tables — rugs are a flexible way to add colour and
pattern to your home.

With bazaar style, the more bold and confident
you are, the better, but when teaming colours and
patterns it's helpful to look for a theme. Choose
to lay Moroccan rugs on your floors — you can
then pick an array of styles and shades, but their
common heritage will pull the look together. Or
draw on a shared colour — bright yellow and blue
Moroccan floor tiles can live happily alongside
cushions covered in Sixties fabric of the same
colour, even though they come from different eras
and countries. Look for one uniting factor, be it
pattern, colour, period or place of manufacture,
to direct your scheme and provide style cohesion.

LIGHTING

We so often overlook lighting when putting together a room, but it's vitally important. It has the power to influence the atmosphere, improve our mood and help us perform daily tasks, from putting on make-up to cooking. Lighting plays a key practical role, but that doesn't mean it must look high-tech. In a bazaar-style home, built-in fixtures are complemented with quirky lamps, mismatched shades and fun fairy lights.

M any modern room schemes place great emphasis on built-in lighting, often featuring rows of recessed spots, track lighting and even bulbs fitted into the floor, but the bazaar look favours a more back-to-basics approach, with plenty of table and standard lamps, wall sconces, chandeliers and decorative shades. This means that, for the majority of your rooms, there's no reason not to light your home as you've furnished it, with a mix of retro, recycled, junk-shop and cheap-chic pieces picked up over the years, at home and abroad.

Before we get excited about the bazaar-style possibilities, here's the science bit. Lighting can be divided into four key types and a successful scheme usually marries them all. General lighting is just that – the central pendant, wall lights, recessed spots and downlighters that create a basic level of illumination. Task lighting helps with specific jobs, from writing to shaving. Examples include an Anglepoise desk lamp or the under-cabinet halogen spotlights in a kitchen. Accent light picks out a specific feature in a room and is about three times brighter than general light – think clip-on lights and spots that fit under shelves to show off a treasured ornament or collection. Natural light needs no introduction, but making the most of what we get is worthwhile.

THIS PAGE *Lights can be practical or, as here, simply decorative. A string of fairy lights hanging around the entrance to a room softens its appearance and, when teamed with small mirror balls, sends pretty sparkles across the space. A striking glass chandelier beyond adds a more grown-up, classical feel.*

OPPOSITE LEFT *Rope lights can be fashioned into signs, creating an illuminated message. It's a kitsch but fun effect, and a strong feature in any room once evening comes.*

OPPOSITE RIGHT *The owners of this house made the contemporary-style sofa themselves and fixed red rope lighting to its frame. When illuminated, the rope lights send a pinky glow up behind the curtains hanging alongside.*

ABOVE LEFT *When the sun shines through the glass bricks in this Moroccan house, it is transformed into squares of colour, cast across the floor.*

ABOVE RIGHT *An ordinary bulb inside a coloured glass shade gives a soft, tinted light to a room.*

OPPOSITE, ABOVE LEFT *A lit tea light softly illuminates the collectables around it.*

OPPOSITE, ABOVE RIGHT *A rope light draped from this vase adds a warm glow to the cool marble of the fire surround.*

OPPOSITE, BELOW LEFT *Flower fairy lights illuminate this butterfly collection and mirror the design of the screen below.*

OPPOSITE, BELOW RIGHT *Fairy lights in an alcove create a relaxing glow, ideal for a bedroom.*

Once you have worked out how each room will be used, choose a mix of light sources to create the right balance between ambience and practicality. You might also keep in mind a few simple tricks that can help make the most of a room's dimensions and features. Make a tall-ceilinged room feel cosier by clustering floor and table lamps together to create low pools of light and by fitting downlighters, which send a wash of light down the walls and draw the eye away from the room's lofty proportions. To make a small room appear larger, position ceiling lights around the borders of the room, not just centrally. To maximize valuable natural light, use minimal window treatments (opt for fine muslin/voile curtains rather than thick velvet, for instance), hang mirrors opposite windows to magnify the light and work in lots of reflective surfaces and pale colours.

ABOVE LEFT *Painted silk lanterns bought in New York's Chinatown make a pretty hanging display – no need for lights inside.*

ABOVE RIGHT *Discs of opaque capiz shell are often used to make jewellery or, as here, elegant light shades. They make a pleasant tinkling sound when caught by the breeze.*

OPPOSITE LEFT *An arcing floor lamp with a dramatic globe shade makes a strong design statement in this living space. Teamed with a striking table lamp on the console behind, the pair create flexible lighting that is bounced back into the room by the large wall mirror.*

OPPOSITE RIGHT *This Moroccan shade made of coloured glass beads throws patterned light around the room and brings a touch of exoticism.*

Once you have a good mix of light sources woven into your room and have worked out where to position them, you're free to have fun with the decorative side of lighting. Beyond the simple drum shades typically fitted to lamps and pendants is a world of fanciful options, from curved plastic shades from the Sixties to tinkling capiz-shell (a product of the oyster industry) pendants and painted paper lanterns. Each will give a simple light its own personality; each will influence the amount of light that escapes into the room. A paper shade allows a mellow, even glow, while a perforated metal lantern from Morocco will throw patterns across your walls. Mix and match shades and bases, particularly if you buy a high-street fitting – give it a bazaar twist with a found shade, or customize a shop-bought shade by pinning on vintage brooches, badges and corsages.

As with furniture and collectables, a bit of TLC can transform a tired second-hand lamp. Metal shades and Anglepoise lights can be spray-painted, ceramic and glass bases can be cleaned with soapy water, and wooden bases can be painted. Lampshades, too, can be dusted down and revamped by stitching on ribbons, buttons or sequins and drums can be recovered in bold new fabrics. If you're buying second-hand, get the electrical fitting checked by an electrician, who can replace frayed flex or faulty bulb sockets inexpensively.

Lighting can be great fun to experiment with and the bazaar look uses the more decorative, flexible types of modern lighting available to good

effect. Rope lights, which are made of hundreds of LED lights inside a see-through cable, look great threaded up stairs or along a mantelpiece. Simple fairy lights come in a variety of colours and decorative shades, and create a pleasing ambient glow. Use them to pick out favourite pictures, thread them around a doorway or wind them through logs in a fireplace.

When you tire of electric light, go back to nature with candles. From simple tea lights to delicate tapers, nothing beats the romance and beauty of a real flame. Better still, candles are cheap and widely available. The fun part is finding a home for them. From an old jam jar to an elaborate candelabra, there are endless ways to bring soft candlelight creatively into your home.

ABOVE *A Russian Impressionist painting gets an extra decorative twist with flower garlands and necklaces draped from its frame. It's a great way to enjoy your jewellery, too — much better than confining it to a box.*

RIGHT *Theming your displays of paintings is a useful technique when it comes to creating an impressive and cohesive wall of images. Here, kitsch 'blue women' and other exotic ladies, all bought at London's Portobello Road market, cover one wall.*

OPPOSITE *Surrounded by framed pictures and photographs, this flat-screen TV, mounted on the wall, could easily be mistaken for a work of art.*

WALL ART

Finding pictures that suit your home and your style can be tricky if you limit your search to the high street, and not many of us have the budget to buy original pieces from galleries. The solution is to scour the second-hand market for oddities and one-offs that you love and will sit well in a bazaar-style home that's packed with unusual pieces. There's an abundance of old art and photography languishing in junk stores, markets and charity shops, often costing very little.

Take your pick, from amateur oil paintings and simple sketches to poignant family photographs of long-gone generations. Old metal advertising panels, touting everything from beer to soap, often crop up at markets or in junk stores. You will also find plenty of postcards from the early and mid-20th century, with photographs or illustrations on the front. They all make great decoration for your walls, many boasting a twist of personal history that makes up for any amateurishness of technique or minor damage.

Mirrors are another wonderful addition to any room. Not only do they look great but they serve a practical purpose, helping to bounce light around, making the space feel brighter and bigger – hang a mirror opposite a window or door for maximum effect. They also create interesting optical tricks. Put a vase of flowers in front of a mirror and they look twice as lush. Position a row of flickering candles next to a mirror for double the glow. Mirrors come in all shapes and sizes. They can have a flat or curved surface, be freestanding or wall-hung, framed with ornately carved wood or finished with a simple bevelled edge. They suit pretty much any place in any room, as they are not bringing an image to the wall or surface on which they rest,

THIS PAGE *Clothes can become art when carefully hung across a wall. Here, a collection of dresses and skirts, made by the fashion-designer owner of this house, lines one wall. If you display clothes in this way, take them down regularly for a brush and shake out, to remove dust and prevent creases.*

OPPOSITE *Art for your walls does not need to be expensive. This corridor is lined with old magazine covers and fashion-shoot images, simply framed. In an adjoining room, embroidery scrolls showing birds, flowers and oriental scenes are hung in a group to make a colourful contrast.*

merely reflecting the colours, light and movement around them. Old mirrors sometimes show their age. Brown spots may appear where the aluminium or silver that coats the glass to make it reflective has perished and the reflection itself may have become misty, but both effects are attractive and testament to the age of the piece.

There are no rules to follow when displaying pictures and mirrors, but if you find yourself with an armful of images, a lot of blank walls and no idea how to put the two together, take inspiration from the bazaars of Iran, Turkey and Morocco. Traditionally, large bazaars like Tehran's Grand Bazaar and the Covered Bazaar in Istanbul were split into corridors, each one specializing in certain types of goods, from spices and carpets to perfumes and precious metals. So use this rationale and group

your images. Hang similar subjects together – portraits, landscapes, horses, still lifes of flowers – or paintings in the same medium, be that oil, charcoal or watercolour. Or group them according to the colour of the frame or the size of the image – a wall of large canvases can look striking, as can one peppered with an array of small photographs in neat black frames.

With the inspiration of real bazaars in mind, remember it is abundance and an organic quality that impresses, not neatness, so cover a wall with images dotted at random. Precision is not essential, so don't worry about lining them up evenly – it is the overall impression that counts. Just mix and match images until you have a combination that pleases your eye. You can add to the arrangement as you find new ones or move them around as your

THIS PAGE *A colourful patchwork canvas fills this chimney-breast wall. It is made from a collection of the patterned collars that Indian men traditionally wear at weddings, stitched together. Its tactile quality suits a bedroom, where sensuality and touchy-feely textiles are welcome.*

OPPOSITE LEFT *Bazaar style loves to tweak the conventional. Here, instead of arranging fresh flowers in a vase, they are casually taped to a wall to make a 3D artwork.*

OPPOSITE RIGHT *Photos, postcards, fake flowers and magazine articles are pinned up to create a lively wall of images. It gives this workstation stacks of personality and visual interest and it's practical, too — the more paperwork on the wall, the less there is cluttering the desk.*

LEFT *Religious imagery can look rather austere, but in this bedroom a holy image is softened by colourful, embroidered quilts and cushions, scattered across the bed.*

OPPOSITE, ABOVE LEFT *A framed painting of a bird is kept company by three smaller images, creating a relaxed display.*

OPPOSITE, ABOVE RIGHT *A funky artwork by Takashi Murakami looks strong above this simple fire surround, while the patterned tiles look like small-scale paintings.*

OPPOSITE, BELOW LEFT *Whether you know the sitter or not, portraits make an arresting addition to any room. This is a portrait of the house's owner, painted by her ex-husband.*

OPPOSITE, BELOW RIGHT *This large, dramatic mirror adds a decorative blast to a white bathroom. Its shelf is home to sparkling jewellery and unusual collectables, while everyday bathroom products are stored out of sight.*

preferences alter. The beauty of this kind of display, where many pictures are hung together, is that no single image has to be especially strong or eye-catching. You are free to pick up paintings and pictures of varying quality simply because they appeal to you, and there is no need to hold out for a masterpiece.

Be resourceful, too. If you find a handsome frame with no image in it, use it to show off a family photograph, postcard, swatch of wallpaper or fabric. Similarly, if you have unearthed an old oil painting without a frame, hang it as a plain canvas – it will look just as impressive. Seek out bargains, too. If

you love mirrors, but your wallet won't stretch to the 19th-century French examples that are so popular today, why not collect British bevelled-edge mirrors from the Thirties and Forties? They are abundant and inexpensive. A quick surf on eBay or a wander around any flea market should reveal several, and they look great hung in groups or propped along a mantelpiece or shelf.

A short time spent reviving old frames reaps rewards. Use a solution of mild detergent and warm water, a soft brush and cotton cloth to ease off dust and grime. You could spray-paint a frame in striking gold or silver, or brush on a coat of eggshell

THIS PAGE *Made by the fashion-designer owner of this house, this canary-yellow gown makes a show-stopping piece of wall art. Combined with a matching PVC-covered sofa and patterned cushions, it creates an uncompromisingly bright scheme.*

OPPOSITE LEFT *Hanging a mirror above a fireplace is a tried and tested look, but here the owner has had fun with the convention by choosing a small, oddly shaped mirror, which looks pleasingly quirky hung on a blank wall. Small Seventies paintings and a deer money box add colour and further humour to this fireplace.*

OPPOSITE RIGHT *Bright colours in this painting are picked up in the flowers arranged in front.*

to refresh it. Grimy glass and mirrors will regain their sparkle with some window cleaner, a soft dry cloth and plenty of elbow grease.

As with every aspect of bazaar style, think laterally, too. Who says pictures need to be hung on walls? They can be appreciated just as well propped against a wall, or sitting on the floor, a chest of drawers or a shelf. Team them with other pieces that you love, or give your picture an extra decorative touch by draping jewellery from its frame, stringing fairy lights around it or tucking party invites or postcards between the frame and glass.

Finally, remember that wall art need not be confined to pictures and mirrors. Hang up beautiful vintage dresses, blouses or skirts. Tape dried flowers to your walls. Pin up a throw, patchwork or gorgeous blanket. Or release your inner Jackson Pollock and make your own mural.

COLLECTABLES *and* DISPLAY

Display is at the heart of bazaar style. It's a look that rejects the minimalist movement of the Eighties and Nineties and its obsession with hiding everything behind sleek cupboard doors. Instead, bazaar style celebrates the beauty of the things we gather up as we go through life, from family heirlooms to jumble-sale finds, holiday souvenirs to birthday gifts. Even those pieces not generally thought of as decorative can be arranged so we appreciate and enjoy them.

THIS PAGE *This beautiful drinks cabinet on elegant legs is home to a selection of vodka bottles and a mixture of collectables. From fake roses to jewelled necklaces, crystal decanters to pretty glasses, it's a showcase of interesting and delicate pieces, intended for permanent display and use – the doors are not meant to be shut. The mirrored back to the cupboard makes the collection seem twice as large.*

OPPOSITE *The windowsill in this Dutch home is covered with objects, some kitsch (a ceramic baby) and some traditional (the photo frames). Blankets and textiles are arranged on the bench in front to be enjoyed, too. Walls are kept plain to prevent the room from feeling too busy.*

THIS PAGE *An old shop bust is a perfect place to hang necklaces, bangles and garlands. This is a great example of how bazaar style takes the things we often tidy away into boxes and pots and displays them creatively.*

OPPOSITE LEFT *This meeting of beautiful fine china and sparkling jewellery is pleasing to the eye but practical, too, as the teapot and cup are used to display and store the brooches, earrings and necklaces.*

OPPOSITE RIGHT *These clothes look too good to be hidden behind wardrobe doors. Hung from an ornate mirror, they add glamour and colour to this bedroom. The mirror and drawers were found in a charity shop and repainted in pastel shades.*

When it comes to what you display in your home, the choice is vast. From tin tea caddies to earthenware cider kegs, from coloured tumblers to costume jewellery, collectables are everywhere. By far the easiest bazaar-style pieces to source, they are fun, often inexpensive and gloriously abundant. In any flea market, boot fair, garage sale or home accessories shop you've ever been into, collectables make up the vast bulk of pieces on sale. And, although you may be looking for a particular item, you're just as likely to see something else that takes your fancy, finding yourself drawn to it for a variety of reasons – nostalgia, sensuality, colour or texture. The important thing when selecting pieces is to trust your instincts and go with your heart. If it's a pineapple ice bucket from the Sixties that appeals to you that day, snap it up – you're sure to find a space in your home for it. Genuine enthusiasm for the object is all that matters.

While they can deliver years of pleasure, collectables also offer instant gratification. Furniture can take time to hunt down or need repairs to be usable. Curtains might need to be altered. Wallpaper must be hung. But collectables bring an instant lift to any room by their presence alone. Team them with other similar pieces to boost a collection or let them stand alone to be fully appreciated. Either way, there's little work involved in gaining enjoyment from a collectable – you only have to look at it.

Collectables aren't just those pieces intended as ornaments. Almost anything can take on collectable status. From the kitchen, old pickle jars and pop bottles, painted flasks or biscuit tins can look lovely grouped together and are easy to find at markets and junk stores. Pieces with a practical purpose, from egg cups to teapots, canisters to cookie cutters, can be decorative, too, so when

you're not using them, display them on open shelves. Non-domestic sources like laboratories, department stores, schools and hospitals shed their excess baggage over the years, and it eventually washes up on the shores of second-hand stores. You might find apothecary jars, scales, globes, cameras, clocks, tills, keys and weights. These can all look decorative, displayed alone or casually sitting amidst a muddle of other well-loved pieces.

Have your bazaar-style radar on when you're abroad, too. The quality and variety of contemporary homewares in overseas shops, particularly in Europe, can be incredibly high, and adding an impressive modern piece to a group of found objects can bring freshness and vigour to a display. Similarly, the injection of some ethnic artefacts or artisan-made pieces will sit well with older finds and second-hand oddments back home, so hit the markets, bazaars and even hardware stores of countries like Turkey and India for good-looking,

ABOVE LEFT *Giving your displays a loose theme can help to create visual cohesion. Here, candlesticks and glassware sit together on top of a cupboard, catching the light.*

ABOVE RIGHT *Decorative Indian candlesticks, arranged in an alcove, don't need to be topped with lighted candles to look beautiful. A jewelled curtain hanging behind adds light and sparkle to the space and frames the display.*

OPPOSITE *Filling a corner of your home with fresh flowers in a mix of brightly patterned, different-height vases creates a strong impact. Here, the blooms and their decorative vessels add welcome colour to the grey-painted dresser and walls.*

well-made gear, from woven baskets and metal lunch boxes to colourful tea glasses and plates.

When it comes to displaying your collectables, play around with the objects you have, trying out different groupings until you find a mix that pleases. One of the delights of bazaar style rests in giving unusual pieces a centre-stage position; in teaming the conventional with the curious, the simple with the ornate. Theming your displays can help. Glass bottles and vases, metal tins and pots, black-and-white pieces – the possibilities are endless. Make your theme narrow (flower-patterned teacups), or broad (any item of silverware); whatever your approach, this method will help you sort through your collectables and find harmonious ways of displaying them.

An extension of this thematic approach is to create a collection purposefully, hunting down ceramics from a particular pottery, maker or area,

for example, or gathering specific items, from salt and pepper pots to brass candlesticks. The added bonus to this approach is that it makes every trip to a market, fair or interiors shop more exciting – the thrill of finding another piece for your collection is great. Looking for a specific item or class of item gives direction to your search, too, helping you to navigate your way through the sea of objects laid out on each stall.

While it's fun to create collections or themed displays, it's the innate flexibility of collectables that is so appealing. So, once you have a display established, don't sit back and let it stagnate. Remember to add to it, move its components around or swap them with pieces from another room. Put some items away in a cupboard, hiding them for a few months so that you can enjoy them afresh when you reintroduce them to a room. Forget buying a new chair or repainting the walls;

rearranging your collectables is the fastest way to give a room a facelift – and it costs nothing.

To help show off your finds, choose open shelves, glass-fronted cabinets and dressers. Decorative side tables will give you space to create small arrangements. Look out, too, for those more unusual pieces that are a good shape to show off specific collections. A dressmaker's dummy could be draped with your favourite necklaces or a vintage dress, a huge bowl could hold an assortment of colourful doorknobs or pretty pebbles.

Rethink every room of your house, too. No space is too small for a cluster of objects. In fact, making an unusual location or forgotten corner home to a handful of pieces brings it to life. The unexpected pleasure of seeing a pretty object in an overlooked nook makes you appreciate it all the more. Glass tea-light holders can perch on top of window frames, a string of colourful fake flowers

ABOVE LEFT *Black, white and grey appear in the cabinet these collectables are arranged on and on the pieces themselves, for a display that's easy on the eye.*

ABOVE RIGHT *Painting shelves the same colour as the wall they hang against is a clever way to make the collectables on them stand out, or – as with the pieces on the bottom shelf – almost disappear.*

OPPOSITE LEFT *Picture frames and, as here, the glass-fronted door of a cabinet are good places to tuck a photo or postcard.*

OPPOSITE RIGHT *This jewellery is far too pretty to hide away and instead takes on a display role by being draped over a dressing-table mirror.*

ABOVE LEFT *A collection of ceramic salt and pepper pots and china money boxes, arranged on curvy, contemporary shelves, brings further colour to this orange-painted kitchen. They were picked up in second-hand shops, fairs and markets by the owner.*

ABOVE RIGHT *A collection of vases sits neatly on this mantelpiece. Turning three of them onto their sides, so the tops face out, creates additional visual variety. The colours in the vases are echoed in the warm sunshine of the painting above, to tie this display together.*

can hang from a doorknob, a row of printer's letters can stand above a door frame.

Whatever the mix of collectables, remember to season it with plenty of humour. Bazaar style doesn't take itself too seriously and is all about having fun with your home's interior. Collectables are a great way to introduce some frivolity into your rooms. Pieces that are over-the-top ornate, luridly coloured or simply incredibly dated can all seem amusing now, while a quirky combination can bring humour to a single piece that, left alone, might not look so appealing. An old stone bust gets a witty new look when topped with a trilby; a slightly naff figurine looks splendid draped with bangles or sporting a fantastic feather hat. Not everyone will appreciate the joke, but that doesn't mean it isn't funny!

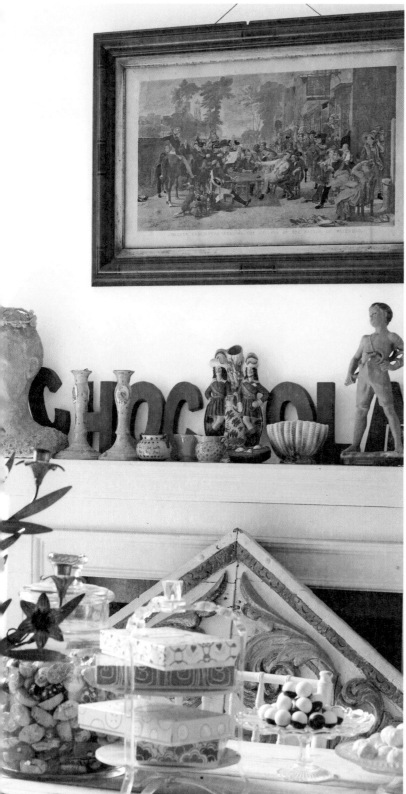

ABOVE *Positioning this figure of a kneeling angel, which could look rather serious on its own, above a shelf of colourful woven baskets and handbags gives it lightness and warmth.*

LEFT *Mantelpieces are ideal places to have fun with display. Figurines, busts, candlesticks, giant letters — they look great together and can be moved around easily to refresh the look. A table spread with sweeties, cakes and chocolates, in glass vases and on elegant stands, completes the relaxed, unpretentious feel of this dining space.*

THIS PAGE *A small alcove in this Moroccan house is the perfect place to fit shelves and create an eye-catching display. A collection of Indian artefacts creates a splash of colour and exoticism in a simply furnished dining space.*

OPPOSITE, ABOVE LEFT *The clear design and strong colours on this coffee pot and milk jug are typical hallmarks of Seventies ceramics.*

OPPOSITE, ABOVE RIGHT *Coloured tea glasses and bowls look beautiful on glass shelves, illustrating how everyday items deserve to be displayed — an idea central to bazaar style.*

OPPOSITE, BELOW LEFT *Even the humble mug or glass — kitchen essentials — can look fantastic when casually stacked on a shelf.*

OPPOSITE, BELOW RIGHT *A collection of metal canisters with bird designs looks highly decorative when grouped together, but has a practical purpose, too, holding kitchen kit and cooking ingredients.*

rooms

THIS PAGE *White walls and flooring create a simple, clean backdrop for this eating space, allowing the collection of paintings to stand out. Old French-style dining chairs with rush seats are brought up to date with brightly coloured cushions, while the table remains neutral thanks to a crisp white cloth with delicate embroidery.*

OPPOSITE *There's an organic feel to the cooking space in this Moroccan home, thanks to the built-in sink, work surface and shelving, made of solid material then rendered to look exactly like the room's walls. Cooking implements are on display and in easy reach, but there's space for some eye-catching artwork on the lofty walls, too.*

COOKING
and EATING SPACES

Cooking and eating used to be two very separate activities. The kitchen was a functional place where food was prepared, while meals were taken in the dining room. Nowadays, with space at a premium and our passion for open-plan living strong, many homes have combined the two areas. Today's busy families and confident cooks prefer to gather in one place to eat, chat, work and relax.

THIS PAGE AND OPPOSITE LEFT *This spacious Amsterdam apartment has a large cooking and eating space where friends and family can comfortably gather. The refectory-style tables are made from recycled timber. The green seats are Robin Day's Polo chair, designed in 1975 as a variation on his classic stacking Polyprop chair. The exposed piping on the ceiling and simple contemporary kitchen units give the space an industrial air, which is softened by the colourful china, glass and baskets dotted around the space. On one wall, fresh flowers are stuck using black tape — an unexpected and amusing way to display your blooms.*

OPPOSITE RIGHT *Stack up coloured glass tumblers on shelves for a beautiful, simple display. Group matching colours together to create a bold effect.*

Combining eating and cooking spaces is practical – everything is on hand, from cutlery to condiments – and sociable, too. What cook wants to be isolated in a back room while their friends relax in the living room? There's also something about the warmth, good smells, colour and activity of a cooking space that draws us to it. Add a table and chairs and it will become the hub of the home.

With its laid-back vibe and emphasis on display, the bazaar look suits this informal, communal way of living. Plates, glasses and cutlery/ flatware are stored on open shelves – no need for friends to ask where to find them. A hodge-podge of cutlery/flatware, gathered over the years, sets a relaxed tone and it can be stored in a simple basket on the table, readily to hand when people gather for a meal. Fabric remnants make pretty tablecloths, old linen tea towels make oversized napkins, comfy cushions soften a bench and jam jars are ideal for holding flowers for the table.

ABOVE LEFT *Tea served from pretty china cups, ornate candlesticks, chocolate truffles arranged on old glass cake stands – a bazaar-style dining space is attractive, relaxing and quirky.*

ABOVE RIGHT *When hung along a wall or arranged thoughtfully on a shelf, kitchen utensils and kit can look beautiful.*

It's a look that instantly puts people at ease and invites friends to unwind.

The bazaar-style cooking and eating space is easy on your wallet, too. There is no need to splash out on matching dining chairs from a high-street store when a mix of junk-shop chairs or a couple of benches will look wonderful. Alternatively, if you lose your heart to a set of modern classics – Saarinen's Tulip chairs or Panton's S chairs, for example – you can economize on the table, choosing a second-hand model that needs a lick of paint to freshen it up, or topping basic trestles with a sheet of toughened glass.

Similarly, by opting for deliberately mismatched china, it's cheap and easy to amass a set large enough to cater for a crowd. Just pick up the components of a dinner service as and when you see them, perhaps sticking to a theme, like floral patterns or geometric designs, or a colourway like shades of cream, or blue and white. Entertaining becomes more relaxing if you know that breaking a plate will not mean the headache of replacing it with an exact match. Instead, see what catches your eye next time you are wandering around a flea market or second-hand shop. Create a set of glasses in this way, too, then have fun picking up non-essentials that will look good, but work hard, too. Biscuit tins, coffee pots, Kilner jars, trays, cake stands and platters are just some of the goodies on offer at markets and vintage stores: often deliciously inexpensive, always brimming with personality.

If you're planning your cooking space from scratch, begin by ignoring the received wisdom that a kitchen area must consist of built-in units. Cooking spaces today are often high-tech, high-cost temples to efficiency and hygiene, packed with

ABOVE LEFT *A retro-style fridge-freezer by Smeg looks good enough to stand on view in this elegant dining space.*

ABOVE RIGHT *Patterned vinyl floor tiles found in a second-hand shop, rustic kitchen units, battered old chairs and a mix of colourful china create an inviting, unpretentious atmosphere in this kitchen.*

THIS PAGE *This home flows like an open-plan space, but with some walls left in place to create pockets of privacy. Here, the kitchen wall remains so that the dining space feels separate and special, and friends are not distracted by cooking clutter or dirty pots when dining.*

OPPOSITE *Although separate from the kitchen, this dining space is far from formal. Lime-green doors on a built-in cupboard unit and striking artwork (some home-grown!) stop the space feeling stuffy. The owners saw the chairs being thrown into a skip outside a social club near their west London home. They got permission to take them and had them reupholstered in blue leather.*

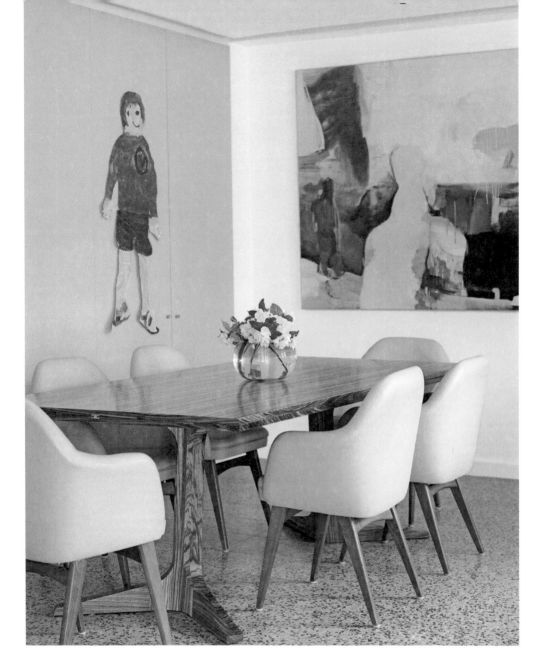

machines and gadgets, but lacking personality. They are one area of the home in which we often stifle our creative instincts, preferring strong lines, sleek units and tough materials such as stainless steel over the more colourful and sensual styles we would choose for other rooms. Modern kitchens can cost a small fortune, too, becoming more of a status symbol than a relaxed place to cook and eat.

However, it doesn't have to be that way. Bazaar style encourages a less designed, more organic approach to kitting out our cooking and eating spaces. Why not choose a few pieces of handsome old furniture instead? Wardrobes, cupboards, glass-fronted cabinets and dressers can hold the bulk of your cookware and crockery, and in a good-sized room you can rely on one big table as your work surface – no need to fit expensive worktops.

If using old furniture that was never intended for life in a kitchen seems a step too far, consider using second-hand kitchen units or furniture

Meal

THIS PAGE *A neat dining space opens off the cooking area in this Moroccan house. A classic Saarinen Tulip dining table is surrounded by retro chairs with a slightly beaten-up look, creating a relaxed modern feel. The lampshade is made from capiz shells.*

OPPOSITE LEFT *Covering a wallpapered wall with perspex is an easy way to give a stylish modern kitchen a bazaar feel and create a practical, wipe-clean splashback at the same time. Vivid orange walls and retro collectables prevent those smart new units looking too clinical, too.*

OPPOSITE RIGHT *The dark panelled walls of this dining space are given extra drama with plenty of orange tones and retro furniture. The glass-topped dining table, moulded chairs and sculptural candlesticks are all retro classics.*

instead. Don't be afraid to ask if you can salvage units from skips, or check your local paper or eBay for them. You may only want to buy a couple, not a whole kitchen's worth, to supplement other freestanding pieces, but this is often possible. You may be lucky and track down some vintage units, too. Kitchen cupboards from the Fifties are highly desirable and very stylish, while individual cupboards from the Forties or Fifties often crop up at markets, complete with frosted sliding doors and melamine finish. Remember to be resourceful, too. If you love the unit, but don't like its finish, remember that you can paint it. Specialist furniture and cupboard paint transforms old melamine in one coat and comes in a range of colours.

Alternatively, stick wallpaper to the doors to give them a fresh, informal makeover.

Bazaar-style cooking spaces often combine built-in with freestanding furniture, to get the best of both worlds. You could line one wall with fitted units and a contemporary sink, then find the remaining storage at markets and fairs. Or have a run of open units made from bricks or concrete and fill them with baskets to house your food and kitchenware. If you're handy with a hammer, or know a man who can, make your own units using reclaimed wood for a rustic, cottagey feel. You could even ditch the doors and string a curtain across the front – a great way to casually conceal large appliances such as the washing machine, too.

OPPOSITE *Design classics like Eero Saarinen's Tulip table and chairs, designed in 1957, work well in a bazaar-style home. Teamed with older pieces of furniture like the console table and a mixed collection of vases, pots and lights, their clean modern lines are softened, but still act as a fresh contrast to the ornate carving and delicate details of their room mates. The huge mirror is an old Venetian piece, bought in New York by the previous owners of this house. When they came to sell their home, they decided it was too heavy and fragile to move, and left it for the next owners, who happened to be friends of theirs, to enjoy.*

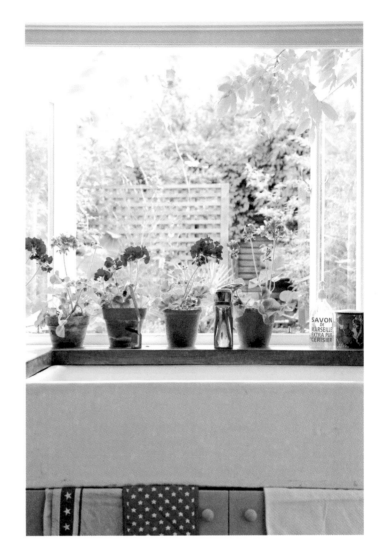

Another smart alternative is to buy inexpensive unit carcasses from a DIY warehouse, then have a carpenter make the doors to your specification. Whatever you do, think creatively and resist the urge to equip your cooking space with uniform fitted units from one supplier. A mix of new, old and reclaimed furniture will bring stacks more personality to the space, and when well planned it will function efficiently, too.

While it is possible to kit out your eating space completely with recycled or second-hand furniture, an up-to-date oven and fridge are a must for all but the most peripatetic of cooks. There's no need to opt for bog-standard white goods, though. There

are several Fifties-style fridges on the market, including Smeg's FAB design, that are good-looking enough to become a real feature of any cooking or dining space. Freestanding ovens, once the preserve of rented flats, are now state of the art and much loved by serious cooks, as are modern range cookers. Their unfitted nature suits a kitchen with odd angles and dimensions. They sit well in a chimney breast, for example, becoming a modern-day version of the ancient hearth.

For all your other kitchen essentials, head to classic bazaar-style sources — salvage yards, second-hand fairs, flea markets. Old butler's sinks (also called Belfast sinks) often turn up at

reclamation yards and cost far less than their new equivalents. They may not have a pristine white finish, but any crazing (cracking in the glaze) adds to their character, and there is no difference in installation or plumbing methods between a brand-new and a reclaimed sink. Although incredibly strong, they can be chipped if hit at the wrong angle by something hard such as a heavy pan, but don't let minor damage put you off. Repair kits for filling and sealing chips are available from specialists.

Lighting is another cooking-space essential, and here a mix of contemporary and reclaimed can work very well. Task lighting is essential in a kitchen. Slicing meat and chopping vegetables become perilous activities in a poorly lit room, while washing up and cooking are frustrating when you can't see what you're doing properly. Installing

modern spotlights under units or using ceiling spots that can be directed so you don't cast a shadow over your work is prudent. The halogen bulbs used in spotlights provide a clear, bright light that is not as warm and yellow as traditional tungsten filament bulbs – ideal for working with.

Once task lighting is in place, you can add ambient lighting for mealtimes and socializing. A row of pendant lights or lanterns hung over a long table adds drama and creates a strong focal point. Small lamps on the table or shelves will also contribute to a soft light. Don't forget candles, either. It's amazing how a table strewn with papers and keys can be transformed into a magical place for a relaxing meal by a sprinkling of candles and tea lights – minimal tidying required.

If your home already boasts a contemporary

THIS PAGE *This outdoor dining space in Morocco looks calm and elegant thanks to a fuss-free scheme of white and pink. A sturdy whitewashed table is flanked by white cushions on a built-in bench and wooden chairs. It makes a fresh backdrop for a mix of pretty pink plates and bowls and simple glasses, all made of plastic and bought in a local market.*

OPPOSITE LEFT *Why serve sugar from its packet when it can find a home in this gorgeous lidded bowl? Plastic tableware like this is cheap and available in any Moroccan market.*

OPPOSITE RIGHT *Although it has a practical use, this pink flask is beautiful, too, and looks lovely displayed next to fresh flowers.*

THIS PAGE *Pasting wallpaper to tired kitchen units and a plain white fridge is an inspired — and inexpensive — way to give them a colourful new look. Although it looks like an old-fashioned design, this paper was recently bought at a DIY warehouse.*

OPPOSITE *A deep windowsill in this Dutch flat is used to house a display of plates and other collectables. The table, too, is home to unusual vases and the bare plaster wall given a humorous lift with a cow-head sculpture, sporting hat, bag and feathers.*

kitchen, there are plenty of ways to give it a bazaar feel. Rather than stash all your pans and crockery away, bring them out so you can enjoy their various colours and shapes. Fit shelves on a blank wall or replace some of the solid unit doors with glass so you can see the cupboard contents. Hang saucepans from butcher's hooks on a chain or metal grid fixed to the wall. Add paintings, photos or some vibrant wallpaper. Create a colourful splashback using reclaimed tiles, or wallpaper protected behind clear perspex or glass. Inject some colour and have fun — even the most neutral modern units and worktops can become full of personality when you work a little bazaar-style magic.

THIS PAGE *Colourful artwork, squashy cushions in vibrant shades, plenty of textiles and throws layered over comfy sofas — this living room marries comfort, style and individuality seamlessly.*

OPPOSITE *White floorboards and walls unite a living space that flows into a dining area. The open-plan space is given further cohesion by patterns, textiles and colours that don't match, but do share a vibrancy and brilliance. Pinks, reds and oranges in particular crop up throughout the scheme.*

LIVING SPACES

Your living space might be the busy heart of the home, or a tranquil haven. It may be the biggest room in your house, or an intimate snug. It might flow, open-plan style, into an eating and cooking space, or be separate from the rest of your home. For that reason, it needs to be flexible and well planned, but personal, too. Bazaar style can deliver all this and more.

Your living room can perform a host of different functions. You may use it as a place to socialize, read, watch TV, relax, work, or all of those things. Once you have identified how you will be using your living space, you can easily plan how to work in colour, lighting, furniture and window treatments that will be fit for purpose as well as bursting with bazaar style.

Think about the walls first – a room's biggest backdrops. Bazaar style's emphasis on displaying objects means that it's often an easy and smart option to keep walls neutral. Let your collectables, rugs, furniture and artwork bring in the colour, texture and pattern. An off-white is a safe choice, but avoid brilliant white, which contains optical brighteners that produce a blue tone, making it look cold and harsh. There are hundreds of off-whites to choose from; use several for a layered effect. You could also leave plaster walls bare or brickwork exposed. If you do yearn to bring colour onto your walls, remember that dark shades will make a space feel smaller, while light will make it feel bigger.

After the walls, floors are the biggest surface in any room. A living space sees a fair amount of traffic, so it needs a hard-wearing surface, but it is also a place of relaxation, so something aesthetically pleasing and kind to bare feet is necessary, too. Wooden floors are a good bet. Wood is attractive, practical and fairly tough without being cold. If you're lucky enough to find good-quality boards hiding beneath a grotty carpet, just clean them with a solution of one part turps, one part meths and one part vinegar before treating them with a sealant of your choice. If some of the boards are rotten, it's easy to add replacement boards. Find a good match at a reclamation yard, or piece in new timber and

THIS PAGE *Black floorboards won't make a room seem dark. Instead, they provide a strong backdrop for furniture and finds. A neutral sofa and armchair are invigorated with an embroidered throw from India and striped cushions from Morocco. The painted wooden chest doubles as storage and a place to rest a drink or book. The foil and glass painting is by Helen O'Keefe.*

OPPOSITE LEFT *Fresh flowers are an instant and natural way to add colour to even the smallest space.*

OPPOSITE RIGHT *Shelves fitted in an alcove can hold so much more than books. Photos, collectables and lamps can all find a home here, creating little framed tableaux.*

THIS PAGE AND OPPOSITE *This airy living space in an Amsterdam house has turned its back on the traditional idea that a sofa and armchairs are essential. Instead, there's a relaxed, North African feel to the room, with low-level seating, floor cushions and tables, all from Morocco, where the owner also has a home. Choosing this kind of seating over a sofa has the added advantage of making the room feel bigger and less cluttered – no bulky furniture in here. A bright scheme of yellow and green looks great – a large space can handle strong colour – while exposed brickwork and bare plaster by the huge picture window add a pleasing roughness to this colourful, well-ordered room.*

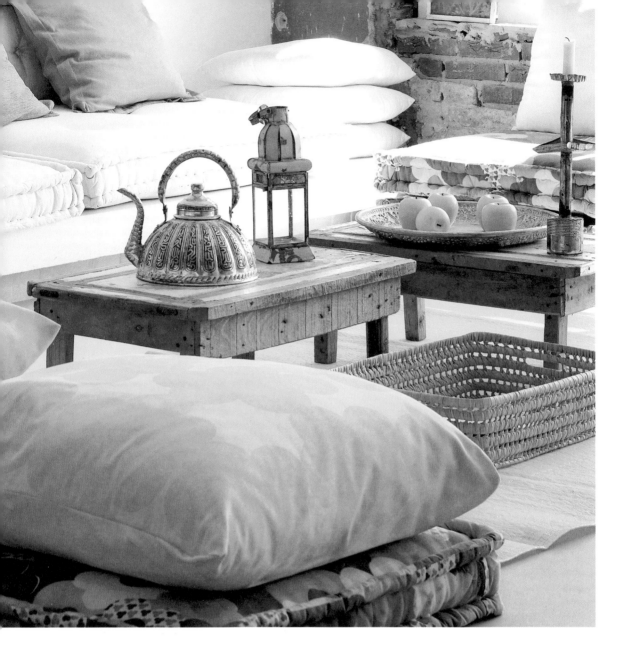

hide it beneath a rug. If you're after a more uniform finish, paint your boards. Dark colours will cover a multitude of knots and blemishes, and if the boards are already reasonably smooth you may not need to sand them – the paint will even out small imperfections. Alternatively, lay new floor boards, which are available in a huge range of timbers, widths and finishes.

Wall-to-wall carpet has fallen out of favour in recent decades, especially in busy downstairs rooms, so if you have hard floors but still crave

carpet's soft feel underfoot, work in a selection of rugs. Toe-tickling sheepskin, animal hides, fluffy flokatis, colourful Moroccan mats – there's plenty of choice. Rugs often show up at markets and fairs. If they look a bit grubby, remember they can be professionally cleaned (or just dry-cleaned if small enough), and don't be put off by a little wear – it adds to the relaxed, bazaar feel. You can also create a rug by having a carpet offcut edged. Called whipping, this service is reasonably priced. Look out for rugs when you go abroad, too, but be careful

THIS PAGE *Fascinating retro and second-hand glass, metallic and perspex pieces fill this airy living space. The owner found the white cube in an Oxfam shop and added black spots to transform it into a dice side table. The leather sofa came from an antiques fair, and the metal storage is an old French school locker.*

OPPOSITE LEFT *This cute sideboard was found in a charity shop. The zebra came from a second-hand market in Brighton, where the owner also has a stall and sells the vintage wallpaper that's standing in the box here.*

OPPOSITE RIGHT *Black and white ceramics are naturally at home alongside black-and-white photographs in monochrome frames.*

when buying animal hides. They are often 'raw', which means they won't wear well – or smell great. Check that the hide has been professionally tanned before buying.

Rugs can be as striking as a piece of art, but they also have a practical function, deadening the sound of footsteps and softening and warming a hard floor. They can influence the impression of space, too. Run striped rugs across a room to make it feel wider, or down a room to make it appear longer. You can also use them to zone a multi-purpose space. For example, a large rug can define the living area in an open-plan layout when you position it under a sofa, coffee table and seating. If a corner of your living room is a place of work, demarcate the work zone by laying a rug under the desk.

When you're picking a rug, you can be bolder in your choice of pattern and colour than you would

LEFT *There's a patchwork theme to this living space. Two Chesterfield-style sofas have been recovered in a mix of colourful, patterned fabrics, which the owner had been collecting for years. She found the bulk of it in a second-hand shop in Bristol. It could look chaotic, but closer inspection reveals that the same fabrics have been used on the same parts of each sofa. This patchwork mix looks glorious and is an inexpensive way to recover a sofa, as anything from old curtains to fabric offcuts can be used, picked up in markets, fabric stores or on eBay. The chimney breast is decorated in the same way, but with wallpaper samples. Neutral walls and a wooden floor anchor the look, while matching lamps, either side of the fire, add symmetry and balance.*

be with carpet, because you can move it easily and a rug is not such a large investment as carpet. You might even want to roll up your rugs and pack them away for summer, or swap shagpile rugs for simple mats when the weather gets warm. Pattern on rugs is a good idea because it hides marks better than a plain finish. Remember that big patterns can act as a focal point, mid-scale patterns provide a degree of visual interest, while small-scale patterns add overall texture.

Living rooms work best when they have a focal point, so before you start positioning your furniture work out what that is. Realistically, it's often the TV, so arrange some seating for viewing it comfortably. Position the rest of your seating at an angle or even facing away from the screen, to encourage other activities such as reading. Traditionally, the focal point in a living room was the fireplace. If yours is unattractive, seek out a handsome original from a salvage yard. The mantelpiece itself can become a

fantastic bazaar-style focal point, dotted with your favourite collectables. Hang a mirror or painting above it, or use wallpaper or a different paint colour to give the chimney breast maximum impact. If the fireplace is a working one, so much the better. No one can resist cosying around a fire on a chilly night. Arrange seating close to it to enjoy the warmth, but be aware of the view from the door – a row of seat backs looks unwelcoming.

Seating is crucial to any living space. Most living spaces work best with a mix of one or two sofas and a few armchairs and chairs. If you're buying a second-hand sofa or armchair, check that the frame is strong and the padding adequate. Having either resprung and restuffed is expensive, so if necessary get a quote before you buy. But if its only fault is a dodgy or dilapidated cover, this can be hidden under throws, sheepskins and blankets.

When it comes to chairs, bazaar-style classics include Lloyd Loom chairs, made from twisted

THIS PAGE *There are some pieces of classic modern design in this living space, including the Lansdowne sofa by Terence Woodgate (from SCP), the Tribeca coffee table by Noguchi, designed in 1944, and the rug by Marni for The Rug Company. They are given a bazaar-style feel through the patterned curtains, quirky Indian cushions and small display of collectables by the window. It's the difference between this being a sleek modern room and a bazaar-style room.*

OPPOSITE LEFT *A hallway is a great place to showcase a knock-out chandelier. So often a neglected part of the house, the hall is much used every day and deserves a little decoration.*

OPPOSITE RIGHT *Two armchairs sit opposite the red sofa (seen on this page), while the boldly patterned Marni rug helps to zone the space and tie it together.*

paper reinforced with steel wire, stackable chairs with colourful plastic seats, squashy armchairs recovered in vibrant fabric, and the humble dining chair in all its manifestations, from a solid farmhouse number in painted pine to a curvaceous modernist example with tubular steel frame and leather seat. A row of cinema seats (look in salvage yards), a low bench or pew, wooden stools or a Moroccan leather pouffe would also look at home. If your room is small, remember that sofas or armchairs that sit on legs will make it feel bigger, because you can see beneath them a little way. Although seating is generally freestanding, don't rule out building some in. A carpenter can, usually quite simply, create a low platform along one wall or in a bay window or alcove, which you can fit with square cushions.

Don't forget the windows when you're styling your living space. The right window treatment offers privacy by night, without blocking out precious natural light by day. Heavy curtains will help insulate your room in winter, while fine muslin can be drawn across to mask an uninspiring view or give some privacy, while still allowing light to filter through. Remember that direct sunlight can bleach a strong colour in a matter of months, so if your room faces south consider roller blinds that can be rolled up completely to protect them from the sun's powerful rays, or choose curtains in a pale colour that won't fade so obviously.

Natural light is invaluable in any room. Maximize it by fitting curtain rails that extend well beyond the window frame, so you can pull curtains clear of the window. Use pretty silk scarves or

THIS PAGE *Wooden cupboard doors and parquet flooring give this room in a Moroccan riad a warmth that's enhanced with splashes of orange on the throw across the sofa, the woven chair and the fresh roses. A tinkling capiz-shell lampshade works well in this high-ceilinged space — a smaller shade could look lost in a room with such lofty dimensions — and adds some decoration and sparkle to this simply furnished corner.*

OPPOSITE, LEFT AND RIGHT *A wall of coloured glass bricks makes an unusual partition in this living space, separating it slightly from the dining area beyond. A brilliant vase is filled with coloured feathers — a non-wilting alternative to flowers that pack just as pretty a punch.*

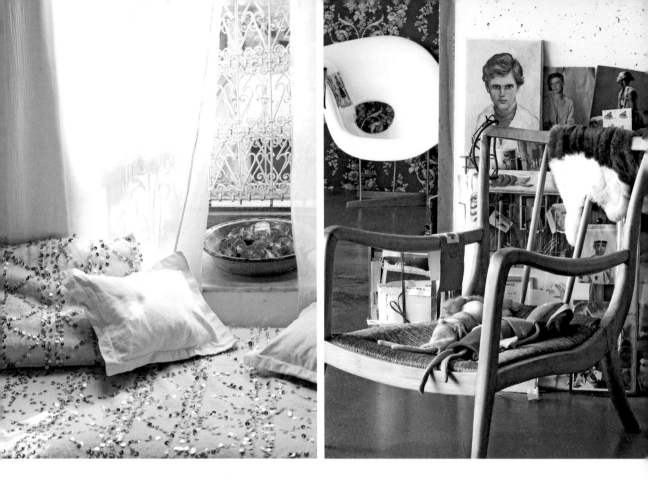

colourful ribbon as simple tie-backs. Paint
windowsills white and keep them clutter-free, then
work in some reflective surfaces near the window
– a fringing of glass beads sewn to the curtain
edges can catch the sun, creating a little sparkle
and increasing the brightness. If you prefer blinds,
rollers do not block out light when completely up,
unlike Roman blinds, which will always obscure
the top quarter of the window.

Flea markets and jumble sales come up trumps
when you're hunting for old curtains. Launder them
in a washing machine – you may have to use one
of the giant-drummed machines in a laundrette/
laundromat – and factor some fabric shrinkage into
your measurements. Keep your eyes peeled for
fabric that could be made into a curtain or blind,
too – a length of vintage lace, muslin/voile or sari
fabric, a tablecloth or bedspread. Hunt down
lengths of old monogrammed linen and have it
made into Roman blinds, string up a beaded

ABOVE LEFT *A Moroccan beaded wedding
blanket has been used here to cover cushions
and some built-in seating, giving it an exotic
feel. Reflective sequins in the fabric catch
the light from the window, creating a little
sparkle and boosting light levels.*

ABOVE RIGHT *Concrete floors can be
painted with floor paint, which comes in
a range of colours. A deep red was used
here. On the wall behind this elegant chair,
disparate images are pinned up casually to
create a low-level display. The white chair
in the background is La Chaise, by Charles
and Ray Eames.*

OPPOSITE *Dark, almost sinister paintings
are balanced with some brightness, via the
floral cushions and reflective glassware on
the console table.*

THIS PAGE *Low-level, built-in seating like this is typical of Moroccan homes, but easy to replicate. Cushions are essential to keep it comfortable — these are covered with a Moroccan wedding blanket.*

OPPOSITE, ABOVE LEFT *A wall of simple shelves creates lots of room to display favourite collectables. These vases pick out the green of the armchair and white of the walls.*

OPPOSITE, ABOVE RIGHT *Two big, comfy armchairs have been recovered in a patchwork of pretty vintage fabrics.*

OPPOSITE, BELOW LEFT *These unusual old chairs sit beautifully in a big bay window area. A child's Ferris wheel toy adds some colour and frivolity to the white room.*

OPPOSITE, BELOW RIGHT *An upstairs landing is an ideal place to paste up a patterned paper, giving this often overlooked part of a home some personality.*

curtain, stick sheets of coloured film to the glass, or get a handyman to build simple shutters that will fold back completely against the wall. Hiding within those plain panes is a bazaar-style window trying to get out.

When you're adding the finishing touches to your living room — the extra bits of furniture or decoration — look out for pieces that appeal to you, whatever room they were originally intended for. A metal garden table can work just as well in a living room as on a patio/deck; a chest of drawers need not live in the bedroom. Choose a mix of large pieces that will need to sit tight once positioned,

and lightweight, flexible items — low tables, stools, baskets, storage boxes, folding screens — that can be moved around, both to refresh the room and to facilitate its different roles. If you're short on space, find pieces that can multi-task. Old metal or wooden trunks or leather suitcases can work as low tables and storage, holding everything from toys to newspapers.

Remember, any piece can be given a bazaar-style revamp. Clean it, paint it, wallpaper it, pepper it with pretty finds or drape it with patterned textiles. Top a simple unit or table with a sheet of patterned wallpaper, covered with glass cut to

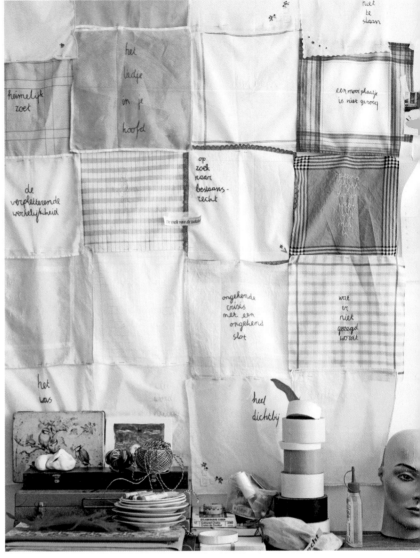

fit. Give a display cabinet extra impact by fitting mirrored glass behind the shelves – your favourite collectables will look twice as good. Keep the look alive by adding, subtracting, mixing and matching. A bazaar-style living space is constantly evolving.

The work space in your home may just be a place where you catch up on paperwork, or you may spend sizeable chunks of your day there. It might be a separate room, or part of a living space or bedroom. Either way, most of us manage little more than some colourful Post-it notes by way of decoration in this crucial area. Add in some

functional office furniture and you have the makings of an uninspiring space. It need not be so. The principles of bazaar style can be applied to a work area just as they can to a bedroom or kitchen, with equally pleasing results.

Let's begin with the desk. Rather than rushing to the nearest furniture warehouse for something practical but generic and dull, try flea markets, junk shops, and even salvage yards, for a desk that is functional and attractive. A small kitchen table with folding sides will fit even the snuggest of spaces, while a reclamation yard might offer up an old

THIS PAGE AND OPPOSITE RIGHT
A chunky old table, second-hand office chair and a good-sized cupboard are the raw materials of any work space. Here, an Anglepoise lamp helps illuminate the sewing machine for close work, while the window provides a good level of natural light. The wall behind the table is decorated with handkerchiefs, which the flat's owner has embroidered with news headlines.

OPPOSITE LEFT *Dressmaking patterns are pinned to the wall in this fashion designer's home.*

THIS PAGE *For dressmaking or needlework, a large table is useful, providing a surface to spread fabric out on. This table is made of old wooden crates and scaffolding poles.*

OPPOSITE LEFT *This lovely old desk has been painted white to soften its appearance. Drawers and cupboards provide storage for paperwork, leaving the surface clear for a few pretty pieces. Instead of a heavy, unattractive office chair, an old dining chair does the job and fits in well. Simple Venetian blinds hung at the window offer some privacy and help diffuse the light.*

OPPOSITE RIGHT *A simple kitchen table is the perfect size for a laptop and suits this small-scale home office. An attractive lamp and blind keep the room fresh.*

workbench or school lab table that would make an excellent workstation.

For seating, pick up a swivelling office chair at a market, or make do with a simple dining chair or folding garden chair that can be tucked away when not in use. Then keep an eye out for office castoffs that can find a new home in your work space. Old plan chests with their numerous drawers offer plentiful storage, while metal filing cabinets can be sanded down and spray-painted to lose their traditional grey finish. Storage boxes, shelves, drawer units, Anglepoise/gooseneck lamps – all kinds of useful work-space kit is languishing in a market or junk shop near you.

Work spaces need to be visually stimulating and inspiring without being cluttered, so function and form must combine. A noticeboard can hold all your notes and invitations, while becoming an attractive artwork, too. For a larger display, line a wall with cork tiles (which can be painted), or apply blackboard paint to one section for the daily to-do list. Always sniff around for an attractive alternative to the mundane. Pencils need not be stored in a dull plastic container; they can live in jugs or Kilner jars. Mesh letter trays can be replaced with shallow wooden crates or wire baskets. Think laterally to make your work space good-looking, but hard-working, too.

THIS PAGE *You can't beat a roll-top bath for glamour. The underside of this bath is painted olive green, a colour picked out in the rug, mirror frame and floorboards. An old occasional table is just the right height to stand next to it, holding a candelabra and fresh flowers.*

OPPOSITE *Bathrooms can be home to all kinds of furniture, chosen for its practicality and good looks. Here, an ornate stand holds towels, while a peg rail, usually found in a hall, is home to bathtime essentials. A colourful rug softens the white-painted floorboards. The lampshade is made from old tins, with holes punched in, bought in Morocco.*

BATHING SPACES

Bazaar-style bathrooms, just like kitchens, don't need to be high-tech or sleek. They can be a mix of the reclaimed and the new, vintage and contemporary. So for a beautiful bathing space with heaps of personality, just give it the classic bazaar-style treatment, displaying daily essentials creatively, mixing in plenty of colour, pattern and texture and tweaking convention here and there. Sofa by the bath, anyone?

The idea of a room in every home dedicated to personal hygiene and grooming is, strictly speaking, a recent one. Most houses built before 1900 didn't have bathrooms, so in just 100 years the bathroom has evolved from a luxury novelty to a universal fixture in the modern home. We've also changed our attitude to them. From seeing bathrooms as a place for a quick wash and brush-up – a functional, often cramped room – we now want our bathing spaces to be sanctuaries. We go there to retreat from the world, locking the door to unwind and rejuvenate. Whether it's a soak in a bath at the end of the day or a peaceful potter as you prepare for work, we expect them to blend practicality with personal style.

Bazaar style works brilliantly in a bathing space, no matter what raw materials – the bath, basin and toilet – you have. It takes a low-tech approach to life, placing emphasis on the character, not the contemporary components of a room, so it doesn't matter if you don't have the latest power shower or sleek mixer taps. If you are completely revamping your bathing space, you can find old basins, baths, taps, toilet bowls and cisterns at salvage yards. Many yards sell metal baths freshly re-enamelled, but if you find one you love with chipped enamel, it's possible to get it recoated by a specialist, either in situ or before you install it. Salvage yards typically sell the classic roll-top bath, with handsome claw feet and painted underside; this is a great way to introduce colour to the room. If you have the space, consider installing one in the centre of the bathroom for the wow factor, and fit double sinks, too – handy for a large family.

THIS PAGE *This bathroom is big enough to accommodate a large French sofa, perfect for perching on while your bath runs or you paint your toenails. A glass-fronted cupboard, found in an antiques shop, was probably intended for life in a kitchen or living space, but is ideal in a bathroom, offering ample storage and room to display colourful bottles and washbags.*

OPPOSITE LEFT *A small old wooden chair, its frame painted pink to match the walls, is topped with towels and an enamel can, used to hold brushes.*

OPPOSITE RIGHT *A patterned towel can take a simple bathroom from plain to pretty in an instant. A beaded hanging basket set, suspended from the towel rail, stores bathing essentials close to the tub.*

THIS PAGE *Woven baskets are a great addition to any bathroom. They bring a welcome splash of bright colour to an often neutral space and offer lots of room to hide your essentials. This lidded basket is from India, while the blue laundry basket is made of woven plastic, so it's waterproof, too – ideal in a bathing space.*

OPPOSITE *This lovely old drawer unit came from a junk shop in Norfolk. It has lots of drawers for hiding away bathroom bits that don't lend themselves to display (cotton buds, razors, toothpaste tubes) and handy pegs for hanging washbags from. On top, old perfume bottles and three floral pictures add another layer of decoration to this bathroom.*

Many bathrooms, particularly in city apartments, don't have a window. Even with one, the bathroom is still a space that requires good, versatile lighting. For night-time ablutions, install wall lights around a mirror or above a basin and rely on a simple ceiling light for when you're bathing or mooching around. Fit a dimmer switch so you can turn it down low for snoozy soaks and light a few candles for lots of atmosphere. Hang a mirror to help bounce light around. A large, plain mirror screwed to the wall behind a basin will also double as a splashback. Freestanding lights are a no-no in a bathroom and wall and ceiling lights should be steam- and moisture-resistant, so you will need to hit the high street or shopping mall, not the flea market, for those.

Don't forget storage. Bathrooms are home to all sorts of daily essentials – from tubes of toothpaste to razors and loo roll – and, unlike the colourful mugs of a kitchen or the beautiful clothes of a bedroom, they are not particularly decorative. So get creative with storage and tuck beauty products and basics away in wall-hung cabinets or a chest of drawers, dug up at a market and refreshed with a coat of paint. Use woven plastic baskets in rainbow colours (try ethnic shops) or large ceramic bowls, too. Remember to pick pieces in moisture-resistant materials such as painted wood, perspex, wicker or glass. Soft woven baskets, invaluable in other rooms, can go mouldy in a bathroom's steamy environment, and metal tins and canisters can rust.

Once you have concealed the unattractive bottles of mouthwash and cans of shaving foam, you can have fun inventing ways to store and display your better-looking bathroom basics. Pile up

ABOVE AND RIGHT *A simple rectangular basin teamed with cool, classic limestone on the walls and surfaces is a great starting point for any bathroom. Here, the mellow look has been revved up with coloured plastic boxes and accessories and an ornate mirror.*

multi-coloured towels on a shelf or bench. Put up peg rails or vintage hooks to hang body brushes and shower gels from. Add a folding garden chair or stool to perch on while the bath fills. Throw in a colourful mat, hang an ornate mirror, pictures to gaze at while you soak, even just a vase of flowers.

ABOVE AND LEFT *The bathroom in this Thirties flat has original panelled walls and a decorative leaded window. To complement, but not overpower, those features, the owner has added a simple, contemporary basin. The perspex cross, hung from the ceiling, adds a splash of red, reflected in the identically shaped cabinet.*

A small white bowl or decorative tile can work well as a soap dish, old jugs and jars can house toothbrushes, and a simple white towel can get a bazaar-style update if you stitch on machine-washable coloured trim.

Look out for retro and vintage pieces that were designed for bathroom life, too. Lloyd Loom laundry baskets, old scent bottles, shaving mirrors, medicine cabinets and first-aid boxes all make regular appearances in junk stores and flea markets. Enjoy mixing pieces from across the eras, whether they were intended for the bathroom or not, to create a space that's functional, but pleasing to all the senses.

THIS PAGE *Bazaar-style sleeping spaces often mix patterns — layering them on a bed means that no single design dominates the space, but all have a chance to be enjoyed. The red print of the Pakistani bedspread and the Indian wall hanging are balanced by crisp white bedlinen with blue embroidery. The cushions add some summer-of-love nostalgia.*

OPPOSITE LEFT *A big leather floor cushion in neutral white is teamed with hot pink and mellow gold cushions, colours that also show up in the rug, basket and child's chair in this pretty bedroom.*

OPPOSITE RIGHT *Pile on the pattern on beds, but look for a theme to help them work together. Soft floral prints cohabit happily here.*

SLEEPING SPACES

While bazaar style is all about mixing objects, colours and patterns, it is not about a design free-for-all. It's a look that loves visual variety, but not visual chaos, and nowhere is this more relevant than in the bedroom. Sleeping spaces need to be restful and calm. Strong colours or lively patterns should be tempered by neutral tones, and pockets of display should be balanced by unadorned space.

ABOVE *This traditional Dutch fabric has a small, detailed pattern that provides background colour when viewed from a distance and lots of visual interest up close. Different examples of the fabric have been cut and stitched together to create a patchwork-effect duvet cover and pillowcases.*

RIGHT *This striking artwork dominates the room and dictates its colours. The white and wine shades of the picture are repeated in the bedlinen, cushions and fluffy throw.*

LEFT *Inexpensive furry blankets from a local market warm up this bed in a Moroccan house. The rich red in the bedding is matched by a rosy red on the walls, creating a warm, enveloping atmosphere. Plain white pillowcases add some freshness and cool the crimson down.*

This means that if you cover your bed with decorative throws and cushions, it's a good idea to keep the walls pale and plain. If you hang patterned wallpaper or dramatic artwork, go for simple white bedlinen. If you group pretty pots and vases on a dressing table, store day-to-day bottles and beauty products out of sight. To keep the room relaxing, an eye for balance is essential.

Finding the visual interest in the objects that naturally belong to each room is a central theme of bazaar style. In the kitchen, crockery and cutlery can take centre stage. In a bedroom, clothes, shoes and jewellery are the stars. They give the room its identity as a place to rest, potter and dress, so it's good to display them. Hang a delicate blouse from a cupboard door or arrange colourful handbags along a mantelpiece. Choose shelves that show off your favourite pieces combined with closed cupboards for the less interesting elements of your wardrobe (nobody needs their socks on display). Open shelves also make it easy to see everything – no more rummaging in the back of the wardrobe. Combining beauty and practicality in this way is something bazaar style does well.

You may choose to keep your sleeping space just that – a place dedicated to sleep. In this case, a bed, bedside table and a couple of lamps are all you need to create a tranquil room. Find a show-stopping bed at an antique shop or heap a mix of beautiful bedlinen from contemporary and vintage

THIS PAGE *A simple mattress on the floor, spread with a beautiful bedspread and brightened up with colourful cushions, is all this Moroccan bedroom needs. Walls are kept clear and neutral, creating a strong sense of height and space. Pebbles gathered on the beach and hung on a string make a fittingly organic decoration for the entry.*

OPPOSITE LEFT *Positioning a bed against a chimney breast has one clear advantage: the recesses to either side can be used for storing bedtime books, magazines and lighting. As with so many bazaar-style bedrooms, simple white bedding is the starting point for this bed, with interest added through a colourful throw.*

OPPOSITE RIGHT *Stools make perfect bedside tables, as they are just the right height to be easily reached when in bed.*

sources onto a simple frame to inject plenty of bazaar style, then keep the room clear. Store your make-up and beauty products in the bathroom and create a dressing area in a spare room or boxroom, where you can hang clothes and keep shoes and other essentials such as a hairdryer. The message your bedroom sends will be clear – this is a space dedicated to sleep, rest and sensuality; very separate from the rest of the house.

Most of us, with space at a premium, make our bedroom work a little harder. The bedroom is generally the place where we keep our clothes, where we sleep, dress and read. While it has great practical purpose, it is also often an area used only in the morning and evening. However, if you choose the essential ingredients – the bed, lighting and flooring – well, work in a modicum of display and plenty of sensual texture, you may be surprised by how much more you use it. Find space for a comfy armchair or chaise and your room can become somewhere you go to read the paper, escape the TV or just gaze out of the window.

The dominant feature of any sleeping space is the bed. We spend about a third of our lives in bed, so the mattress needs to be comfortable. Invest in the best-quality mattress you can afford, then

THIS PAGE *This cosy bedroom has lots of personality, thanks to the pattern-rich cushions and throw across the bed. Small square recesses cut into the wall (there is loft space behind) provide storage for books and a bedtime drink. The pigeon light is by Ed Carpenter.*

OPPOSITE LEFT *There is plenty of pattern in this bedroom, but it shares a loose theme — florals against a white background — to keep the look cohesive. The curtains are made from vintage fabric bought at a market, and the bedside table is from Morocco.*

OPPOSITE RIGHT *Patterned curtains liven up any bedroom. Teamed with white walls and simple bedding, they make a strong, but pretty feature.*

recoup some pennies by picking up a second-hand frame. From old metal hospital beds to French carved wooden beds, there's a style to suit every wallet. Alternatively, buy a simple divan base and layer on floor-skimming sheets, blankets and bedspreads to hide its plain appearance. For a bazaar look with a whiff of nostalgia, find faded eiderdowns and floral quilts, old linen sheets that are gloriously soft, crocheted blankets and embroidered pillowcases at flea markets and vintage shops. They can all be dry-cleaned to refresh them, while cotton and linen sheets can simply be machine-washed. To bring a touch of Morocco or the Middle East to the room, choose strong, saturated colours and ethnic prints on cushions, flat woven rugs and bedspreads. And forget matching sets. A motley collection of bedding looks great and is always ready – grab the first sheets, pillowcases and blankets on the pile and just put them together.

When it comes to storage, the bazaar look favours the freestanding. Furniture that can move around, that is flexible and adaptable, is central to any bazaar-style room. Hunt for pieces with personality – an ornate French armoire, a tall chest of drawers with bun feet, a cavernous blanket box – or buy something cheap that can be simply modified. Remember, when you're looking for furniture, to concentrate on finding the shape you like, not the finish, as it can always be painted, papered or treated to new knobs or handles. To give a plain wardrobe or cupboard a new look, cut out sections of its doors and replace with chicken wire, or remove the door and hang a patterned curtain instead.

In a sleeping space the lighting needs to be gentle, but you will also need some task lighting for bedtime reading or looking in the mirror, and one fairly strong light so you can see to dress on dark winter mornings. If you have a central

ABOVE LEFT *Hanging a beautiful dress or colourful hats and bags from wardrobe doors or a peg rail is an easy way to bring pattern and vibrancy to a sleeping space. It's flexible, too – just hang different clothes every day – and gives the room a strong identity as somewhere to dress and potter.*

ABOVE RIGHT *Shoes and handbags are designed to be decorative, and look great arranged on open shelves. It's also easy to find the pair you want – no rummaging in the back of the wardrobe.*

pendant light, dress it flamboyantly in a glittering chandelier or big, decorative shade, and fit a dimmer switch so you can control its brightness. Supplement it with table lamps on chests of drawers, a mantelpiece or dressing table, so you can vary the mood. Gather bases in a range of styles, then crown them with pretty patterned shades so they look as good switched off as on. You will certainly need a light by your bed. Wall lights that can be angled to shine on your book are practical, but a low lamp on a bedside table will do just as well; after all, it only needs to be bright enough to illuminate the pages – you don't want glare.

THIS PAGE *This bedroom has all the ingredients of a gently feminine space – twinkling chandelier, floral cushions, fresh flowers, pretty blinds – but without looking fussy or girly. A bold throw from Pakistan, mismatched cushions and the knocked-about feel of the chest of drawers give the room a lived-in air that's far from prissy.*

There is room for some decoration and display in a sleeping space, but, as we have discussed, balance is key. This is a place where too much visual interest can be detrimental, creating an over-stimulating environment that is hard to relax and sleep in. To avoid this, choose pieces that can multi-task, performing a useful function while also adding a dash of bazaar style. Use an old glass cake stand to pile your make-up on and save space on your dressing table at the same time. Find old suitcases or hatboxes that can hold shoes or bags.

Look out for ottomans, wooden chests or wicker blanket boxes that offer lots of storage space and, when scattered with cushions, a place to sit, too. Take care not to let the room or surfaces become cluttered, though. A bazaar-style sleeping space has just the right combination of your personal things with clear space, colour and neutrality to ensure a good night's rest.

THIS PAGE AND OPPOSITE RIGHT
An embroidered quilt from Cath Kidston, clothes and necklaces hanging on show, and bright bedside tables picked up in Morocco — all give this space a relaxed personality. The owner, who collects vintage fabric, has customized the lampshades by stitching on small panels of patterned material.

OPPOSITE LEFT *Peg rails don't just belong in halls. In this ensuite bathroom, a rail holds shower caps and pretty bags.*

OUTDOOR LIVING

Gardens used to be just for the green-fingered, but these days we're more likely to treat them as an extra room. They can perform numerous roles – a play area for kids, somewhere to entertain or a tranquil place to relax – and by borrowing ideas from indoors, perhaps even the furniture, textiles and cushions, too, you can make your outside space into an extension of your home.

ABOVE LEFT *This garden is given a blue scheme, thanks to a grass-style umbrella and a painted shed. Simple wooden furniture gets lots of bazaar style with cushions and a tablecloth made from fabric remnants and beading, designed by the house's owner.*

ABOVE RIGHT *A Chinese parasol and French wrought-iron chairs and a table are the centrepiece of this small town garden. Built-in benches, bordering the garden, supplement the seating without cluttering the space. The fabric covering all the cushions is deliberately bright and contemporary, to give this courtyard a modern twist.*

There are many ways to bring some bazaar style to your outdoor space, be it a balcony, city courtyard or rolling country patch. When it comes to planting, potted plants are ideal. Hundreds of plants, herbs and small shrubs work well in pots rather than planted in a bed, and grown this way they are movable, too, so you can shift them around to create zones and generate visual variety. In a small city garden, which may be paved or decked entirely, they are the best way to introduce some natural colour and texture, while in a larger patch they can soften the hard lines of patio borders and create pockets of interest.

Flea markets are great places to look for tubs, troughs and containers. You will also spot plenty of vessels that can be reinvented as plant pots. Old metal pails, tea caddies, baskets, wooden crates, butler's sinks: anything that can hold compost can nurture a plant. If the material allows, pierce holes in the bottom for drainage, but before you get carried away and plant up an old tin bath, consider its weight, especially if you are putting pots on a balcony or roof terrace. Large vessels or those made from heavy stoneware can weigh a great deal. Is your space strong enough to support a full container? Could you move it if you wanted to? If not, you can buy wheeled caddies for heavy pots.

Seating is essential in even the smallest outdoor space and it's worth considering building it in – a great way to create some structure in your outside room. Just build a low platform along a garden or house wall and cover it with quilts, rugs and cushions. You could also get some storage built in underneath so you can stash furniture away easily

ABOVE LEFT *Standard wooden garden furniture can get a bazaar feel by being liberally covered with a bright throw from India and chunky cushions in stripy fabric and pretty English florals by Cath Kidston. The parasol is also Indian.*

ABOVE RIGHT *A pile of cushions softens the built-in bench in this Moroccan roof terrace. The bold, almost retro fabrics are actually contemporary Moroccan designs, picked up in a local market. The surprise of finding them here, instead of the more predictable kilim fabric one usually sees in Moroccan homes, adds to their appeal.*

ABOVE LEFT *A shot of brilliant magenta makes a bold but pleasing contrast to this chair's leafy, natural surroundings.*

ABOVE RIGHT *Create a simple garden bench along one wall by laying planks across stacked-up breeze blocks, then pile on cushions for comfort. These are from Morocco.*

OPPOSITE *Design tricks that work indoors can do just as well outdoors. Hanging a mirror will make an enclosed garden seem bigger and brighter, while painting garden walls can influence the mood of the space. Introducing colour with cushions and an Indian throw is an easy way to lift the feel of a outside space, too – no need for flowering plants.*

at night or in the winter. Supplement this with flexible seating and a table, too. Old deckchairs, wooden benches and tables, French café chairs and tables in wood or wrought iron, and wicker armchairs – all turn up regularly at flea markets and in junk shops. Remember that, unless the furniture you find is weatherproof or made of hard-wearing wood such as teak, it will need to be stored under cover to protect it from the elements. You could choose pieces that will work indoors, too, or create some outside storage space – a brightly painted shed, perhaps – to keep them in good shape until spring comes.

Reclamation yards are good hunting grounds for garden furniture, too, and you may also find garden tools, interesting ornaments, planters and paving stones. Do check that the retailer makes sure that all items for sale have been legally sourced (see Source Directory for a list of reclamation yards and other salvage outlets). There has been a big trade in stolen garden furniture, ornaments and statuary in recent years, so check the provenance before buying.

Colour is at the heart of bazaar style, and in an outdoor space that need not come just from the planting. In a small city garden, paint fences or walls in rich Moroccan shades of turquoise, rose and sand. Look out for painted Lloyd Loom furniture or warm up plain wooden chairs with colourful cushions. If your garden is overlooked, draw the eye away from the surrounding buildings by laying bright floor cushions, colourful rugs and simple rush mats on decking, lawn or paving. Create visual cohesion by finding colour themes, too, just as you would indoors. Match foliage and flowers to a favourite garden rug or picnic mat,

zingy deckchair fabric or a patterned hammock, parasol or awning.

Finally, you can use some of the bazaar-style tricks and techniques that work well indoors in your outdoor space, too. Hang a large mirror on a boundary or house wall to increase the sense of space and light in an enclosed garden. Drape baubles and glitter balls from trees to catch the sunlight and create some sparkle. Dot a table with favourite ornaments and jugs filled with freshly picked flowers. Then set the scene for romantic evening dining with plenty of candles. To prevent them blowing out, pop them into tea-light holders or storm lanterns, metal lanterns or old jam jars. If biting insects are spoiling your supper, light citronella candles – their sharp, lemony smell will keep any bugs at bay.

THIS PAGE *This outdoor pool is given a frivolous feel with pink-painted walls and seating. Woven plastic baskets, a bathroom staple, work brilliantly here, too – they are capacious, colourful and water-resistant.*

OPPOSITE, ABOVE LEFT *Bazaar style believes in layering on pattern and colour. The outside is no exception, so even if your garden is brimming with flowers there is room for a few more blooms on cushions.*

OPPOSITE, BELOW LEFT *Candles come into their own during twilight mealtimes. Pop them into storm lanterns, old bottles, metal lanterns, or tea-light holders, to protect the flames from gusts.*

OPPOSITE, ABOVE AND BELOW RIGHT *Any material that can reflect the sunlight will add sparkle and visual texture to your outdoor space, whether that be coloured glass tumblers or shiny metal balls, hung from a branch.*

SOURCE DIRECTORY

Most towns and cities have plenty of charity shops, junk/thrift shops and flea markets. Venture a little way out of the city centre and away from its chain stores to find them. Check in local papers, too, or on community noticeboards for listings of weekend boot sales, jumble sales or summer fairs.

Selina Lake
Interior Stylist
(+44) 07971 447785
www.selinalake.co.uk
www.selinalake.blogspot.com

RECLAMATION YARDS & SALVAGE

Caravati's
104 East Second Street
Richmond, VA 23224
(+1) 804-232-4175
www.caravatis.com
Materials and architectural details from old buildings.

Château Domingue
3615 West Alabama Street
Houston, TX 77027
(+1) 713-961-3444
www.chateaudomingue.com
Architectural elements, furnishings, and accessories.

LassCo
30 Wandsworth Road
London SW8 2LG
(+44) 020 7394 2100
www.lassco.co.uk
Architectural antiques, salvage and curiosities.

Salvage One
1840 West Hubbard
Chicago, IL 60622
(+1) 312-733-0098
www.salvageone.com
Architectural artefacts.

Salvo
www.salvo.co.uk
Directory of UK suppliers of architectural salvage.

FURNITURE & ACCESSORIES

Anthropologie
To find a store near you, visit www.anthropologie.com.

Select mix of often vintage-inspired one-of-a-kind home accessories and decorative details.

Aram Store
110 Drury Lane
London WC2B 5SG
(+44) 020 7557 7557
www.aram.co.uk
Long-established store selling modern furniture, lighting and accessories by big design names like Ron Arad and Verner Panton.

Baileys Home and Garden
Whitecross Farm
Bridstow
Herefordshire HR9 6JU
(+44) 01989 561931
www.baileyshomeandgarden.com
Furniture and storage made from recycled materials, old-fashioned household products, taps and sinks, lighting and garden gear, all available by mail.

Couverture
188 Kensington Park Road
London W11 2ES
(+44) 020 7229 2178
www.couverture.co.uk
An ever-changing source of vintage finds, plus covetable one-off designer pieces for the home, women's and kids' clothing and accessories.

Design Within Reach
Call (+1) 800-944-2233 or visit www.dwr.com to find a store near you.
Modernist furnishings traditionally found only in designers' showrooms.

Graham & Green
4 Elgin Crescent
London W11 2HX
(+44) 020 7243 8908

Also stores in Regent's Park Road, King's Road and Chiswick.
www.grahamandgreen.co.uk
Big range of furniture from around the world, plus gifts, lighting, and accessories for every room in the home. All available to order online.

Josephine Ryan Antiques
(+44) 07973 336149
www.josephineryanantiques.co.uk
Furniture and home accessories, often with a French feel.

Labour and Wait
85 Redchurch Street
London E2 7DJ
(+44) 020 7729 6253
www.labourandwait.co.uk
Timeless, functional products for daily life, from enamel colanders to feather dusters. Mail order available.

Live Wild at Heart
30A Pimlico Road
London SW1W 8LJ
(+44) 020 7221 6434
www.wildatheart.com
Homewares including vases, cushions covered in vintage fabric, and bedlinen.

The Moroccan Bazaar
(+1) 972-599-2933
www.themoroccanbazaar.com
Moroccan chandeliers, lanterns, lamps, sconces, and other accessories, including room dividers and mirrors.

Newel Art Galleries
425 East 53rd Street
New York, NY 10022
(+1) 212-758-1970
www.newel.com
A six-story building housing antiques from many periods.

RE
Bishops Yard
Main Street
Corbridge
Northumberland NE45 5LA
(+44) 01434 634567
www.re-foundobjects.com
Mail-order company selling interesting homewares, new and found, from the UK and abroad.

Richard B. Arkway
59 East 54th Street,
Suite 62
New York, NY 10022
(+1) 212-751-8135
www.arkway.com
Antique maps, globes, atlases, rare books, and other curiosities.

SCP
135–139 Curtain Road
London EC2A 3BX
(+44) 020 7739 1869
www.scp.co.uk
One of the largest outlets for contemporary design in Britain.

Snooper's Paradise
7–8 Kensington Gardens
Brighton BN1 4AL
(+44) 01273 602558
www.northlaine.co.uk/snoopers-paradise
Over 90 different stalls selling antiques, collectables, vintage jewellery, clothing and retro.

Thorsten Van Elten
Unit 14–15
10–14 Hollybush Gardens
London E2 9QP
(+44) 020 7739 7237
www.thorstenvanelten.com
Interesting and innovative furniture, lighting and accessories by young designers, including Ed Carpenter's Pigeon light.

Zara Home
To find a store near you, visit
www.zarahome.com
*Furniture, bedding, lighting
and accessories, often with
a Moorish feel, from this
Spanish brand.*

WALLPAPER & TEXTILES

Blink Décor
www.blinkdecor.com
*Online retailer of wallpaper
designs from antique glam
to modern chic.*

Blissliving Home
To find a store near you, call
866-95-BLISS, or visit
www.blisslivinghome.com
*Modern, globally inspired
bedding, pillows, and other
homewares.*

Cole & Son
Ground Floor 10
Chelsea Harbour Design
Centre, Lots Road
London SW10 0XE
(+44) 020 7376 4628
www.cole-and-son.com
*Striking wallpapers made
using traditional techniques,
including block printing and
flocking.*

Larusi
Unit 14, The Dove Centre
109 Bartholomew Road
London NW5 2BJ
(+44) 020 7428 0256
Open by appointment.
www.larusi.com
*Specializes in the weavings of
the Berber tribes of Morocco,
including rugs, cushions,
throws and blankets.*

Neisha Crosland
(+44) 020 7657 1150
www.neishacrosland.com
*Decorative wallpapers and
furnishing fabrics in stylish,
contemporary designs.*

Secondhand Rose
230 5th Avenue, suite 510
New York NY 10001
(+) 212-393-9002
www.secondhandrose.com
*Huge collection of wallpapers
from Victorian to 1970s.*

Timorous Beasties
384 Great Western Road
Glasgow G4 9HT
(+44) 0141 337 2622
&
46 Amwell Street
London EC1R 1XS
(+44) 020 7833 5010
www.timorousbeasties.com
*Surreal and provocative
textiles and wallpapers.*

**www.wallpaperfromthe70s.
com**
*Geometric designs from
Germany.*

www.5qm.de
*Danish site selling original
wallpapers from the Fifties,
Sixties and Seventies.*

FLOORING

Dar Interiors
Studio 3T, Cooper House
2 Michael Road
London SW6 2AD
(+44) 020 7731 6388
www.darinteriors.com
*Specialists in Moroccan
tiles for floors and walls,
handmade by artisan
craftsmen employed on a fair-
trade basis. Also furniture,
lighting and home accessories.*

Flor
(+1) 866-952-4093
To find a store near you, visit
www.flor.com
*Souk Chic rug tiles, composed
of vibrant patchwork pieces of
Turkish and Persian rugs.*

International Paints
(+44) 08444 817 817 for
advice and stockists.
www.international-
paints.co.uk
*Supplier of specialist paints
and primers, including an
interior floor paint suitable
for use on concrete, wood and
stone floors. Also tile paint,
furniture and cupboard paint
and radiator aerosol paint.*

The Rug Company
Showrooms in London UK
and the United States. Visit
www.therugcompany.info

*Wide range of high-quality
designer rugs, many by famous
designers.*

Woven Accents
8674 Melrose Avenue
West Hollywood CA 90069
(+1) 800-222-7847
www.wovenonline.com
*Antique and new handwoven
rugs from India, Persia, and
Morocco.*

WALL ART

**Ana Drummond and
Helen O'Keefe**
*Work by these two artists is
available at*
Cross The Road
141 Portland Road
London W11 4LR
(+44) 020 7727 6760

Takashi Murakami
www.takashimurakami.com
*Learn more about Japanese
artist Murakami here. Find his
work through online art
dealers or eBay.*

FLEAMARKETS & FAIRS

UK

For national listings of car
boot sales and markets, go to
www.carbootcalendar.com.
London has numerous
excellent markets, from
small back-street markets
selling bric-à-brac to the
large, famous markets like
Portobello Road and
Greenwich, where
everything from antiques
to crafts and clothes is
available. Find listings of
all London's markets at
www.londonmarkets.co.uk.
Outside London, there are
hundreds of regular antiques
fairs and markets around
the country. Particularly
good ones include those at
Newark (Notts), Swinderby
(Lincs), Ardingly (East
Sussex) and Goodwood
(West Sussex). Visit
www.antiques-web.co.uk
for detailed listings.

Near London, Tring Market
Auctions in Hertfordshire
holds weekly sales. Visit:
www.tringmarketauctions.
co.uk.

US

You'll want to visit flea
markets, antiques sales,
and auctions. Some famous
U.S. fairs are listed below.
You can also check out
www.fleamarket.com for a
national directory of flea
markets, swap meets, and
trade days.
When traveling, the local
Chamber of Commerce can
be an excellent source for
info on rummage sales.

**Brimfield Antique &
Collectible Show**
Route 20, Brimfield
MA 01010
www.brimfieldshow.com
*This celebrated flea market
runs for a week in May, July,
and September.*

**The Manhattan Art and
Antiques Center**
1050 Second Avenue at
56th Street
New York, NY 10022
(+1) 212-355-4400
www.the-maac.com
*Large emporium selling
an eclectic mix of period
furniture, paintings, porcelain,
chandeliers, and more.*

Picc-a-dilly Flea Market
796 West 13th Street (Lane
County Fairgrounds),
Eugene, OR
(+1) 541-683-5589
www.planeteugene.com/
fleamarket.htm
*Antiques, crafts, and
collectibles, including fabrics,
every Sunday, except in July
and August.*

Rose Bowl Flea Market
1001 Rose Bowl Drive
Pasadena, CA 91103
www.rgcshows.com/
rosebowl.aspx
*Everything from retro kitsch to
fine antique furniture, on the
second Sunday of each month.*

PICTURE CREDITS

Key: **a**=above, **b**=below, **r**=right, **l**=left, **c**=centre.

All photography by Debi Treloar

Page 1 l the home of Joanne Cleasby, stallholder at Snooper's Paradise, Brighton; **1 cl** the home in Amsterdam of the stylist/artist Reineke Groters; **1 cr** www.juliaclancey.com; **1 r** private house in Amsterdam, owner Ank de la Plume; **2 row one: l** the London home of David and Jaz Bushell of Drapestar; **cl** the London home of Nikki Tibbles, owner of Wild at Heart–Flowers and Interiors; **cr** Alan Higgs Architects; **r** www.juliaclancey.com; **2 row two: l & cl** the home of Netty Nauta in Amsterdam; **cr** www.juliaclancey.com; **r** Madeleine Rogers of Mibo; **2 row three: l & cr** the London home of Sam Robinson, co-owner of The Cross and Cross The Road; **cl** www.juliaclancey.com; **r** the London home of Nikki Tibbles, *ibid.*; **2 row four: l** www.juliaclancey.com; **cl** the London home of Sam Robinson, *ibid.*; **cr** the home of Netty Nauta, *ibid.*; **r** the London home of the owners of Hope & Greenwood, Miss Hope and Mr Greenwood; **4–5 a** the home of Isobel Trenouth, her husband and their four children; **5 c** www.juliaclancey.com; **5 b** the London home of Louise Scott-Smith of www.lovelylovely.co.uk; **12 row one: l & r** the home in Amsterdam of the stylist/artist Reineke Groters; **cl** the home of Isobel Trenouth, *ibid.*; **cr** the London home of Sam Robinson, *ibid.*; **12 row two: l** the London home of Sam Robinson, *ibid.*; **cl** private house in Amsterdam, owner Ank de la Plume; **cr** the home of Isobel Trenouth, *ibid.*; **r** the London home of Louise Scott-Smith, *ibid.*; **12 row three: l** Alan Higgs Architects; **cl** the home of Isobel Trenouth, *ibid.*; **cr** the London home of Sam Robinson, *ibid.*; **r** Madeleine Rogers of Mibo; **12 row four: l** the London home of Nikki Tibbles, *ibid.*; **cl** private house in Amsterdam, owner Ank de la Plume; **cr** the home in Amsterdam of the stylist/artist Reineke Groters; **r** Riad Chambres d'Amis in Marrakech (B&B), designed and owned by Ank de la Plume, decorated in co-production with Household Hardware and Rutger Jan de Lange; **14 & 15 b** the home of Netty Nauta, *ibid.*; **15 a** the home of Sarah O'Keefe, co-owner of The Cross in West London; **16 l** the home in Amsterdam of the stylist/artist Reineke Groters; **16 r & l** the London home of Nikki Tibbles, *ibid.*; **17–18** www.juliaclancey.com; **19 a** the home of Joanne Cleasby, *ibid.*; **19 bl** Alan Higgs Architects; **19 br** the London home of Nikki Tibbles, *ibid.*; **20 l** the London home of Sam Robinson, *ibid.*; **20 r** the London home of Louise Scott-Smith, *ibid.*; **21 l** the London home of the owners of Hope & Greenwood, *ibid.*; **21 r** the London home of Nikki Tibbles, *ibid.*; **22** the London home of Louise Scott-Smith, *ibid.*; **23 l** the home of Netty Nauta, *ibid.*; **23 r** the London home of Louise Scott-Smith, *ibid.*; **24 l** the London home of Nikki Tibbles, *ibid.*; **24 r** the London home of Sam Robinson, *ibid.*; **25** the London home of Nikki Tibbles, *ibid.*; **26 & 27 r** the home of Sarah O'Keefe, *ibid.*; **27 l** the home of Isobel Trenouth, *ibid.*; **28** the London home of Sam Robinson, *ibid.*; **29 l** private house in Amsterdam, owner Ank de la Plume; **29 r** Riad Yima, owned and designed by Hassan Hajjaj and managed by Abdelghafour Benbadryef, is available to rent; **30 l** the home in Amsterdam of the stylist/artist Reineke Groters; **30 r** the home of Sarah O'Keefe, *ibid.*; **31** the home of Netty Nauta, *ibid.*; **32** the London home of Nikki Tibbles, *ibid.*; **33** Alan Higgs Architects; **34 l** the London home of Louise Scott-Smith, *ibid.*; **34 r** Madeleine Rogers of Mibo; **35 l** the home of Joanne Cleasby, *ibid.*; **35 r** Riad Chambres d'Amis in Marrakech, *ibid.*; **36 a & bl** the home in Amsterdam of the stylist/artist Reineke Groters; **36 br** the home of Isobel Trenouth, *ibid.*; **37** the London home of Louise Scott-Smith, *ibid.*; **38 l** private house in Amsterdam, owner Ank de la Plume; **38 r** Dar Beida and Dar Emma, available to rent – www.castlesinthesand.com, interior designers Emma Wilson

and Graham Carter; **39** the home of Isobel Trenouth, *ibid.*; **40–41** the home in Amsterdam of the stylist/artist Reineke Groters; **42–43** the London home of David and Jaz Bushell, *ibid.*; **44 l** private house in Amsterdam, owner Ank de la Plume; **44 r** Alan Higgs Architects; **45 al** the London home of Nikki Tibbles, *ibid.*; **45 ar** the London home of David and Jaz Bushell, *ibid.*; **45 bl** the London home of Sam Robinson, *ibid.*; **45 br** Riad Chambres d'Amis in Marrakech, *ibid.*; **46 l** the home in Amsterdam of the stylist/artist Reineke Groters; **46 r** the home of Isobel Trenouth, *ibid.*; **47 l** Alan Higgs Architects; **47 r** Riad Chambres d'Amis in Marrakech, *ibid.*; **48 l** the London home of Sam Robinson, *ibid.*; **48 r** www.juliaclancey.com; **49 l** the London home of Nikki Tibbles, *ibid.*; **50** www.juliaclancey.com; **51** the home of Netty Nauta, *ibid.*; **52 l** private house in Amsterdam, owner Ank de la Plume; **52 r** the home of Netty Nauta, *ibid.*; **53** Alan Higgs Architects; **54 al** the home in Amsterdam of the stylist/artist Reineke Groters; **54 ar** Madeleine Rogers of Mibo; **54 bl** the London home of the owners of Hope & Greenwood, *ibid.*; **54 br–56** www.juliaclancey.com; **57 l** Madeleine Rogers of Mibo; **57 r** the London home of Sam Robinson, *ibid.*; **58** the home in Amsterdam of the stylist/artist Reineke Groters; **59** www.juliaclancey.com; **60** the London home of Sam Robinson, *ibid.*; **61** www.juliaclancey.com; **62–63 l** the London home of Sam Robinson, *ibid.*; **63 r** Riad Chambres d'Amis in Marrakech, *ibid.*; **64 l** the London home of Sam Robinson, *ibid.*; **64 r** www.juliaclancey.com; **65 l** the home of Joanne Cleasby, *ibid.*; **65 r** Madeleine Rogers of Mibo; **66 l** the home of Joanne Cleasby, *ibid.*; **66 l–r** the London home of Nikki Tibbles, *ibid.*; **67** the London home of the owners of Hope & Greenwood, *ibid.*; **68** Riad Chambres d'Amis in Marrakech, *ibid.*; **69 al** the home of Joanne Cleasby, *ibid.*; **69 ar** private house in Amsterdam, owner Ank de la Plume; **69 bl** the London home of Louise Scott-Smith, *ibid.*; **69 br** the home in Amsterdam of the stylist/artist Reineke Groters; **70 row one: l** the London home of Sam Robinson, *ibid.*; **cl** the home of Sarah O'Keefe, *ibid.*; **cr & r** the London home of Louise Scott-Smith, *ibid.*; **70 row two: l & cr** the home of Sarah O'Keefe, *ibid.*; **cl** Dar Beida and Dar Emma, *ibid.*; **r** the London home of Sam Robinson, *ibid.*; **70 row three: l** Riad Chambres d'Amis in Marrakech, *ibid.*; **cl** the London home of Sam Robinson, *ibid.*; **cr** the London home of the owners of Hope & Greenwood, *ibid.*; **r** the home of Isobel Trenouth, *ibid.*; **70 row four: l & r** the home in Amsterdam of the stylist/artist Reineke Groters; **cl** the London home of Louise Scott-Smith, *ibid.*; **cr** the home of Sarah O'Keefe, *ibid.*; **72** the London home of Sam Robinson, *ibid.*; **73** Dar Beida and Dar Emma, *ibid.*; **74–75** private house in Amsterdam, owner Ank de la Plume; **76 l** the London home of the owners of Hope & Greenwood, *ibid.*; **77 r** the home of Isobel Trenouth, *ibid.*; **77 l** www.juliaclancey.com; **77 r** the London home of Louise Scott-Smith, *ibid.*; **78–79** Alan Higgs Architects; **80** Dar Beida and Dar Emma, *ibid.*; **81** the home of Joanne Cleasby, *ibid.*; **82–83** the home of Sarah O'Keefe, *ibid.*; **84–85** Riad Chambres d'Amis in Marrakech, *ibid.*; **86** the home in Amsterdam of the stylist/artist Reineke Groters; **88–89** the London home of Sam Robinson, *ibid.*; **90–91** the home of Sarah O'Keefe, *ibid.*; **92–93** private house in Amsterdam, owner Ank de la Plume; **94–95 l** the home of Joanne Cleasby, *ibid.*; **95 r** the London home of Nikki Tibbles, *ibid.*; **96–97** the home of Isobel Trenouth, *ibid.*; **98–99** Alan Higgs Architects; **100–101** Riad Chambres d'Amis in Marrakech, *ibid.*; **102** the London home of Nikki Tibbles, *ibid.*; **103 l** Riad Chambres d'Amis in Marrakech, *ibid.*; **103 r** the home in Amsterdam of the stylist/artist Reineke Groters; **104 al** the London home of Nikki Tibbles, *ibid.*; **104 ar** the London home of Nikki Tibbles, *ibid.*; **104 bl** the London home of the owners of Hope & Greenwood, *ibid.*; **104 br** the home of Isobel Trenouth, *ibid.*; **105** Riad Chambres d'Amis in Marrakech, *ibid.*; **106 l** the home of Netty Nauta, *ibid.*; **106 r–107** the home in Amsterdam of the stylist/artist Reineke Groters; **108** private house in Amsterdam, owner Ank de la Plume; **109 l** the London home of the owners of Hope & Greenwood, *ibid.*; **109 r** Madeleine Rogers of Mibo; **110** the home of Sarah O'Keefe, *ibid.*; **111** the home of Isobel Trenouth, *ibid.*; **112 l** the London home of Sam Robinson, *ibid.*; **112 r** the London home of Louise Scott-Smith, *ibid.*; **113** the home of Sarah O'Keefe, *ibid.*; **114** the London home of Sam Robinson, *ibid.*; **115–116** private house in Amsterdam, owner Ank de la Plume; **117** the home of Joanne Cleasby, *ibid.*; **118** the home of Sarah O'Keefe, *ibid.*; **119** the London home of Sam Robinson, *ibid.*; **120 l** private house in Amsterdam, owner Ank de la Plume; **120 r** the London home of David and Jaz Bushell, *ibid.*; **121** Riad

Yima, *ibid.*; **122** Dar Beida and Dar Emma, *ibid.*; **123 l** Riad Chambres d'Amis in Marrakech, *ibid.*; **123 r** private house in Amsterdam, owner Ank de la Plume; **124** the London home of Louise Scott-Smith, *ibid.*; **125–126 l** the home of Isobel Trenouth, *ibid.*; **126 r** the home of Netty Nauta, *ibid.*; **127** the London home of Sam Robinson, *ibid.*; **128–129** the home of Isobel Trenouth, *ibid.*; **130–131** Alan Higgs Architects; **132 l** the home of Isobel Trenouth, *ibid.*; **132 r & 133 l** the London home of Sam Robinson, *ibid.*; **133 r** Dar Beida and Dar Emma, *ibid.*; **134 l** Alan Higgs Architects; **134 r–135** the home of Sarah O'Keefe, *ibid.*; **136 al** the home of Isobel Trenouth, *ibid.*; **136 ar** the London home of Sam Robinson, *ibid.*; **136 b–137** Alan Higgs Architects; **144 cl** the home in Amsterdam of the stylist/artist Reineke Groters; **144 cr** the London home of Louise Scott-Smith, *ibid.*; **144 r** www.juliaclancey.com.

ARTISTS, DESIGNERS AND RETAILERS WHOSE WORK IS FEATURED IN THIS BOOK

www.castlesinthesand.com
+44 (0)776 8352190 (UK mobile)
+212 (0)679 65386 (Moroccan mobile)
For commissions, email emma@castlesinthesand.com
38 right; 70 row two centre left; 73; 122; 133 right.

www.chambresdamis.com
12 row four right; 35 right; 45 below right; 47 right; 63 right; 68; 70 row three left; 84–85; 100–101; 103 left; 105; 106 right–107; 123 left.

Joanne Cleasby at Snooper's Paradise
7–8 Kensington Gardens
Brighton BN1 4AL
01273 602558
1 left; 19 above; 35 left; 65 left; 66 left; 69 above left; 81; 94–95 left; 117.

www.drapestar.com
2 row one left; 42–43; 45 above right; 120 right.

Reineke Groters, stylist and artist
reineke.groters@zonnet.nl
1 centre left; 12 row one left & right; 12 row four centre right; 16 left; 29 left; 30 left; 36 above & below left; 40–41; 46 left; 54 above left; 58; 69 below right; 70 row four left & right; 86; 103 right.

Haberfield Hall
Haberfield Hall is available for hire as a photographic location for both still and moving film. Please contact Helene Field at

Shootspaces.
020 7912 9989
07880 636473
enquiries@shootspaces.com
www.shootspaces.com
4; 5 above; 12 row one centre left; 12 row two centre right; 12 row three centre left; 27 left; 36 below right; 39; 46 right; 70 row three right; 77 right; 96–97; 104 below right; 111; 125–126 left; 128–129; 132 left; 136 above left.

Alan Higgs Architects Limited
173 Seymour Place
London W1H 4PW
020 7723 0075
fax 020 7724 4290
mail@alanhiggsarchitects.com
www.alanhiggsarchitects.com
Team: Alan Higgs, David Weston-Thomas, Richard Nicholls
Sliding fabric panels in drawing room and living room by Ketcher and Moore; lighting design in drawing room by Light IQ.
2 row one centre right; 12 row three centre left; 19 below left; 33; 44 right; 47 left; 53; 78–79; 98–99; 130–131; 134 left; 136 below–137.

Hope & Greenwood
Purveyors of Splendid Confectionery.
www.hopeandgreenwood.co.uk
2 row four right; 21 left; 54 below left; 67; 70 row three centre right; 76 left; 104 below left; 109 left.

www.householdware.nl
1 right; 12 row two centre left; 12 row four centre left; 29 left; 38 left; 44 left; 52 left; 69 above

right; 74–75; 92–93; 108; 115; 116; 120 left; 123 right.

www.juliaclancey.com
1 centre right; 2 row one right; 2 row two centre right; 2 row three centre left; 2 row four left; 5 centre; 17–18; 48 right; 50; 54 below right–56; 59; 61; 64 right; 77 left.

Lovelylovely
020 7482 6365
info@lovelylovely.co.uk
www.lovelylovely.co.uk
5 below; 12 row two right; 20 right; 22 & 23 right; 34 left; 37; 69 below left; 70 row one centre right & right; 70 row four centre left; 77 right; 112 right; 124.

Mibo
tel and fax 08700 119620
info@mibo.co.uk
www.mibo.co.uk
2 row two right; 12 row three right; 34 right; 54 above right; 57 left; 65 right; 109 right.

Riad Yima
52 Derb Aarjane – Rahba Lkdima
40 000 Marrakech – Medina
+212 (0)24 39 19 87
and
LaRache Boutique
30–32 Calvert Avenue
London E2 7JP
020 7729 7349
hassanhajjaj@gmail.com
All the artizanas: Riaka and Saida (Morocco), Ekram (London)
29 right; 121.

Snooper's Paradise
7–8 Kensington Gardens
Brighton BN1 4AL
01273 602558
nic@internetdropshop.co.uk
6–11.

The Cross and Cross The Road
141 Portland Road
London W11 4LR
020 7727 6760
fax 020 7727 6745
2 row three left & centre right; 2 row four centre left; 12 centre right; 12 row two left; 12 row three centre right; 15 above; 20 left; 24 right; 26–27 right; 28; 30 right; 45 below left; 48 left; 57 right; 60; 62–63 left; 64 left; 70 row one left & centre left; 70 row two left, right & centre right; 70 row three centre left; 70 row four centre right; 72; 82–83; 88–89; 90–91; 112 left; 114; 118; 119; 127; 132 right & 133 left; 134 right–135; 136 above right.

The Turquoise Island
222 Westbourne Grove
London W11 2RJ
020 7727 3095
fax 020 7792 8302
flowers@wildatheart.com
www.wildatheart.com
2 row one centre left; 2 row three right; 12 row four right; 16 right; 19 below right; 21 right; 24 left; 25; 32; 45 above left; 49 left; 66 right; 95 right; 102; 104 above right.

INDEX

Figures in *italics* refer to the illustrations and captions.

ACKNOWLEDGMENTS

I would like to thank Alison Starling for realizing my Bazaar Style book idea and for giving me such an exciting opportunity. A massive thank you to Debi Treloar for all her beautiful photography, friendship and humour, for being such great company in Brighton, Bristol, Amsterdam and especially Morocco (and for the Caipirinha introduction!). Many thanks to Joanna Simmons for her witty and interesting words. A massive thank you to all at Ryland Peters & Small for their hard work and dedication to this project, including Jess Walton, Amy Trombat, Clare Double, Gemma John and Leslie Harrington. I would like to personally thank all the generous people who gracefully welcomed us into their beautifully Bazaar homes.

On a personal note I would like to thank all my friends who have wished me luck and my lovely family for all their support and encouragement. Thank you, Mum, Dad, Aimee and My Dave.
Selina Lake

Joanna Simmons' thanks go out to Alison Starling, for giving her the opportunity to write this book, to editor Clare Double for her diligence and good-naturedness, to Selina Lake for dreaming up the idea and making it come to life, and to Steve, for his patient support.